The Ultimate Guide to a Successful Business Website

The Non-Technical Person's Handbook For Hiring a Web Designer and Managing the Creation, Design and E-marketing of a Business Web Site

Note: The principles advocated in this book cannot be guaranteed to bring you financial success with your Web business. Hard work, a good product and service, reasonable prices, and the best of customer relations are equally important.

Note: Website addresses change all the time. I have included website addresses (also known as URLs) in a number of places within this book. Some may not work by the time you read this since the website owners may remove their site or change the location of content I reference. Bear this in mind when attempting to find sites listed here.

This book is dedicated to my dad Terry and my son Brandon.

Contents

Section 3

THE PLANNING AND IMPLEMENTATION OF A SUCCESSFUL BUSINESS WEBSITE

Introduction

Why this book is so important to you

You are a time-challenged business person. You lack highly technical computer skills but realize you need a new business website. This book is for you.

Perhaps you need to transform your idea into a brand new, fully functional, money-making business website. Or maybe you need to revamp an under-performing and lifeless existing website. Either way, you're greatly increasing your chances for success by reading this book.

If you don't already have a website, you're going to need one, that's for sure. If you have an outdated site that embarrasses you, you can't afford to leave things as they are any longer.

You can suffer through the entire website building process and be massively disappointed with the end result, blind to the details, ignorant of website fundamentals, and full of regret for the amount of money you spent. Or you can ensure that you'll save time and money, understand what goes into a great website, have a relatively easy time with the whole process, be thrilled with the final product, and end up with a successful website that helps you achieve all your business goals.

This book's entire purpose is to help you achieve this. You will learn how to transform a simple idea or an old and dead site to a new website that greatly improves your life and business. You will learn how to hire the right Web design company or person for your project. And you will learn what constitutes a successful website so you can be involved in the process and understand and suggest what is needed to achieve your website's goals.

Treat the preparation and production of your new website in the exact same way as you would the planning and construction of your new family home.

When you set out to build a new house to live in, you don't go into the project blindly, ignorant of the process and choices, and lacking a clear vision of the house you want to own. You realize that you and your family will be living in your new house every day. You wouldn't think of handing a big check to the first home builder you meet, would you? You wouldn't choose a builder at random, trusting them to know what they're doing and hoping they will build exactly what you want without working with them, would you? Don't make this mistake with your business's website either.

Some people think that hiring a "technical" high school or college kid to build their site is the best bargain. Maybe the kid is taking a Web design course and wouldn't charge much.

I ask people who are considering this approach two questions. First, is your business important to you and do you expect to make money with the site? I then ask if they would entrust a school kid who's taking a home-building course to build their new family home. These questions get the person thinking.

"But it's just a simple a website I need and besides, kids these days are whizzes at computer stuff. Right?"

I then ask them, "How serious are you about your business? Do you have a strong desire to create a *successful* business website that achieves all your goals?" I point out that most eighteen-year-olds don't have the marketing, design and technical skills to create anything you would want to associate with your business name. After they think about it a while, most people realize that when it comes to Web design, what they put into it is what they'll get out of it. They understand that the online world is no different from the "real" world.

You get what you pay for. A website is the twenty-first century equivalent of a twentieth century brick and mortar business. Using shortcuts will create big problems for you down the line. You certainly wouldn't hire a high school kid to build your new store on Main Street, would you?

Planning is everything. As a Web designer, developer and marketer myself who has owned and operated a Web design business for many years, I've been asked countless times if I could help someone with their first website or re-vamp an existing one. Usually they'll tell me that they have little money to spend, have no idea what they want or need, don't really know "how websites and the Internet work," and are not too particular about who builds the site for them. They just know they need one.

At that point I always wish I had a book to hand them that explained why knowledge, foresight and planning are vital to the success of such an important facet of their business. So I decided to write the book you're reading now.

A business website today is as important as the office building or plant of yesterday. You need to have a website built for your business. Treat it like you were having your store built on Main Street of your city. This mindset will put you ahead of your competition.

You get what you pay for. You also get what you put into it. This means that if you give the project no thought and plan on spending no more than $100, expect the Web equivalent of a lemonade stand made out of cardboard.

By putting no time or effort into planning or learning what you're undertaking, conducting no research, failing to scrutinize potential website builders and leaving it up to strangers to create whatever they want, you will be the owner of an overpriced disappointment that misses the mark completely. The resulting website could actually make you look worse than not having one at all.

The poorly planned website could end up costing you more money that it makes, wasting your time and souring you to the entire Web world permanently. You're going to have to live with your website every day. You want it to be great. If it is, it can radically change your business for the better.

But since you're reading this book, none of the above predictions need to apply to you. You can end up with a successful website for a fair price, working for you within a reasonable time frame.

Even if this isn't your first business website and even if you have a website but are planning on hiring a Web designer to re-vamp it, arming yourself with the knowledge found in these pages will make you better equipped to hire the right people and oversee the project with educated eyes. It will make your life much easier.

There is a place for $100 websites, to be sure. If you want to test a new product or service, investing a small amount of money at first may be the prudent thing to do. But if you're serious about getting online, don't dabble. Do it right the first time. Or if you're serious about making drastic improvement to an existing site, then commit to the process. If you're about to have a website built that you expect to significantly help your business and make you money, then read on.

Note: The term "Web Designer" is a misnomer. Building a website requires much more than just graphic design skills; it involves technical skills, marketing skills and Internet business knowledge as well. A lot more on this later. Realize that when I use the term "Web designer" *or* "Web Design Company" *in this book, I mean a* "Web vendor," *a person or group of people who have a range of Internet skills and know how to design, code and market websites from start to finish.*

The world is moving online. The number of households and companies that have Internet access is increasing daily. Broadband is steadily expanding as well. According to eMarketer.com, 82 percent of American households are online in 2007, and by 2010 they predict the reach will be over 90%. They also predict that by 2010 more than 88 percent of U.S. households will have broadband access. (Data from the U.S. Department of Commerce).

An "entry barrier" is the need for costly or rare resources that can prevent people from starting a business. Let's look at the barrier to entry for people who want to start an online business. Actually, there really is no barrier to entry. Anyone can start an online business with almost no investment.

For a few dollars anyone can build a website and start selling information, goods or services online. It's nothing like the old days when starting a business meant procuring a business loan, finding and renting a physical location, hiring employees and complying with many regulations, all before anything is sold! As easy as it is to start an online business, without careful planning it's just as easy to fail.

4

Hundreds of thousands of new small businesses start up every year. A recent issue of *Entrepreneur Magazine* states that around 672,000 new businesses were created in 2005 alone, the largest business creation rate in U.S. history.

You can be anywhere in the world and start a Web business. And because of low costs, many people are doing it. And more importantly, it's not the big businesses that are reaping the rewards of the Web. Individuals and businesses with only a handful of employees will benefit the most from the Internet.

This is because there is a massive market fragmentation going on today. The days of the big brands are gone. According to master marketer Seth Godin in his book, *Small is the New Big,* "The number of megabrands and their value (in terms of the premium consumers are willing to pay) is shrinking, and fast.... and the number of microbands is exploding."

Internet Marketing Guru John Reese (www.income.com) in his e-book, The Rebirth of Internet Marketing, has this to say:

> It's not the big companies that are going to wreak havoc across the Internet Marketing landscape...It's the millions upon millions of men, women, and now even children from all over the world that are rushing to start their own online business. They are creating the revolution.

So it's a good thing that you're considering building a new website. The questions are, How are you going to be different from the millions of small companies and entrepreneurs who are also building new websites? And How can your website stand out from the crowd and ensure that it fully accomplishes your unique business goals?

Do you want an overpriced, flimsy online hut hacked together by an incompetent Web designer that makes you look bad and scares customers away? Do you want the entire website building process to be as painful as a fifteen-hour labor? Or do you want a gorgeous, professional website that does everything you want, makes you and your business look professional, trustworthy and reliable, that makes you money, and is a joyful and smooth experience to build? Do you want to pay a fair price or do you want to get overcharged? Do you want your website to take a matter of weeks to be built or take a better part of a year? Do you want to have a site that breaks down three months after it's built or one that continues to make you profits year after year?

For everything you learn in advance, for every minute you put into understanding the Web before you embark on the production of your own site, you will improve your chances of success tenfold.

Read on to learn exactly how to do it right.

Who Am I? Why Should You Listen To Me?

I am a professional Web designer, programmer and marketer. I own the consulting firm, Oak Web Works, LLC (http://www.oakwebworks.com). I earn my entire living online. I have helped countless individuals and organizations get online for the first time. I have also seriously improved existing Web properties for clients all over the world.

I own and operate e-commerce websites and blogs that generate millions of dollars in sales each year. I have built hundreds and hundreds of websites. I've created and implemented a multitude of e-marketing campaigns for businesses in a wide range of industries. And I have programmed many Web applications that are on production websites today, churning up data as you read this.

I've been a webmaster for high-tech start-ups and large organizations. I've worked as a Web person in some capacity before, during and after the Internet bubble. I have done Web work for MIT, Intel, and *New York Times* best-selling authors. I have been hired by traditional marketing and advertising firms to help them with their clients' online endeavors. I buy and sell Web properties. I currently design, build, manage and market many of my own websites today.

More important than all of this is the value I place on education above all else. I'm not talking about college classes teaching concepts and skills that are woefully behind the cutting edge of today's Internet. Colleges and universities are barely hanging on to the knife handle. I'm referring to books and online resources. I am a voracious reader. I read Web and business books constantly. I also study and soak up as much knowledge as I can online. From forums, tutorials, e-books, and blogs, to online marketing and design organizations, I spend literally thousands of dollars every month learning the most up-to-date and leading edge Web information that exists today. I also regularly attend Web design and marketing seminars, either online or in person, that are taught by the recognized leaders of the Internet world. Now I want you to benefit from all my studying.

Keep in mind that the Internet, technology and online marketing are constantly changing and evolving, so although the information contained in this book is as relevant as possible for today (2008), things change fast in the online world. The good news is that most of the concepts presented here are website fundamentals that will be around for a long time to come.

Who will benefit from this book?

Whether you're a lone entrepreneur with no technical skills and needing a new website, a small business owner who needs an existing site re-vamped, or an employee tasked with finding a Web designer or Web design firm to build a new company website, the more information you're armed with, the better your chances of making this endeavor a success.

If you're new to the Web and have zero experience with building or managing a website, but have some experience surfing the Web, this book's for you. If you're somewhat of a Web expert perhaps as a programmer, an e-marketing specialist, or a Web designer, then this book is for you, too.

Wherever you are on the spectrum from novice to guru, many nuggets of information contained in these pages will make your job much easier. I am confident that here you'll find advice and recommendations you have never thought of before. This book is a one-stop shop for planning and implementing the creation of a successful business website.

You may be good at design or marketing, but making the right hire is a skill unto itself. By the time you're done reading this book, you can have that skill.

As I have mentioned, the barrier to entry for online businesses is so minimal now that almost anyone anywhere can start a business online. You could be a budding entrepreneur primed for starting and running a new Web business. You could be an employee of a company with an idea for starting a business and the realization that a website is paramount to your success.

Or you could be a mom looking for a way to work from home during odd hours to make a living. You could be the owner of a business who is fed up with your existing site and needs a next-generation website that will bring in much more money than it will cost you to build it.

You could also be an employee who is in charge of the company's Web presence. Maybe your company doesn't have a website yet, and you've been given the assignment to get one built, cheaply and quickly. Or you could be heading up the initiative to re-vamp your firm's outdated website. If your company needs a website and you want to look like a hero, you too will greatly benefit from reading this book.

Whatever your mission, whatever your need, if you work with websites or see the creation of success-building websites in your immediate future, you will be glad you found this book.

What's in this book for you

Before you buy a new car, build a house, or take on a new career, you will do your research in advance. The same approach works with Web design, even if you hire a person or business to put your pages together for you. The reality is that the more you know in advance, the better equipped you'll be to hire the right Web vendor.

If you're building a new house, it would be obvious to you that the more you know at the onset of the project, the more money you will save, the less time you will spend, and the chances that the house will come out the way you want it to will be high.

Furthermore, by knowing and examining all your options in advance you'll be much better equipped to ask the architect and builders to produce the house that best meets your individual needs. The same goes for a website.

In Section One I will explain to you what a Web presence entails. I will make it crystal clear what a website should be and what it should do. I will teach you what makes a website successful. I will explain the various options you have and prepare you for knowing what to ask potential Web vendors.

You'll learn the difference between an e-commerce site and a blog. You'll also learn all the pieces that make up a fully functional website, from a domain name to a hosting provider.

In Section Two, we'll get to the nuts and bolts of hiring the right person or firm for you. You'll learn how to plan the project correctly and how to determine what kind of website will best accomplish your business goals. I'll explain the differences between hiring an individual, freelance Web designer or a larger Web development firm. Then you'll discover how to differentiate various services and how to discern who is an honest and qualified person to hire.

Checklists with explanations on making the right hire before you pull the trigger will be provided. When you've made your decision, you'll need to know how to close the deal with confidence that you're not being overcharged. You'll have a written plan and a proper contract to sign.

Section Three will show you how to plan and implement the creation of a successful business website. You'll learn how to work together with the Web vendor you hired to map out and construct your new website.

The last chapter will explain to you that having a website built is just the beginning and that you'll need to market it properly online to get the most out of it. I'll explain to you what types of marketing you ought to consider doing and why.

If you're already familiar with what makes up a website, skip to Section 2.

SECTION 1

THE FUNDAMENTALS OF EVERY WEBSITE

Understanding what makes up a basic website and the types of website choices you have before you begin your project will enable you to plan a website that will best achieve your goals. With this basic knowledge, you'll be able to be more accurate in requesting the tasks you'll need a Web vendor to handle for you.

In this section you'll learn about the kinds of websites available today and what each can do for you. You'll learn what is needed to go from an abstract idea to a live and useful website. You will also learn the basic elements that every website needs.

Armed with this knowledge, you'll be able to speak intelligently with potential Web vendors and will be better able to choose the right one for you. Once the choice is made, you'll be well equipped to help your Web vendor build the site you need to accomplish your online business goals.

Chapter 1

Websites and What They're Made Of

The Anatomy of a Website

When the Web began there was only one main type of business website. I call these first websites "brochure-ware sites."

The site was basically a digital version of the company's printed brochure. It had a few links and probably contained more content than the one-page printed brochure, but it didn't do anything special. It may even have contained the company's catalog, but there was virtually no interactivity. And these sites did not add any revenue to the company's bottom line.

Today there are many types of websites. When you click around the Internet, you're likely to see purely informational websites, community information, forums, e-commerce sites and blogs. Most of them can be monetized. In other words, most websites today can make money.

Information Websites

Information sites are just that—websites that provide information. They are the descendants of the original brochure-ware websites. Often the owners of information websites offer advertising to earn revenue. CNN.com, Britannica.com and WebMD.com are examples of information websites. They are content-rich with original information that is constantly updated. These sites generally have a lot of pages, and they often sell advertising.

If you can produce quality, original content, then you can use an information website to build a regular readership. This in turn will attract advertisers who will regularly pay you to show their ads to your website viewers.

Community and Forum Websites

Websites that people can join, participate in and interact with other members are community or forum websites. These websites allow members to post questions or comments to existing threads or discussions or start new topics (threads) by making a post that they expect to be answered. These types of sites are the ancestors of Web 2.0., Google Groups, Yahoo Answers, and WebmasterWorld.com are examples of community forum websites. If a forum has many members, it can also attract advertisers.

E-Commerce Websites

You are probably already familiar with e-commerce websites. An e-commerce website is simply a site that allows users to purchase products and pay for them with credit cards online. The website owner gets the order and drop ships or directly ships the purchased product to the customer's door. Amazon.com is a perfect example of an e-commerce website.

Blogs

Blogs are often considered part of the Web 2.0 phenomenon. However, blogs have become so popular and useful to their creators that they deserve their own category. Because blogs are new, often misunderstood, and an excellent way to start your online presence without needing technical skills, I am going to spend a little more time fully explaining blogs.

The word "blog" is short for "Web log" or "weblog," and the "blogosphere" is the online blog world, some parts of which are hyperlinked extensively to each other.

Here is the Wikipedia definition of blog:

Blog is short for weblog. A weblog is a journal (or newsletter) that is frequently updated and intended for general public consumption. Blogs generally represent the personality of the author or the Website.

I recommend that you read lots of people's blogs to learn what blogs are. Go to your favorite search engine and type in the word "blog" and the subject you're interested in. You will most likely find hundreds of examples.

Blogs have become a way in which regular, non-technical people can post information to the Web as easily as they can access it.

Online businesses can benefit from blogging by taking advantage of a vehicle for easily posting new, original, and business-related content on a regular basis.

Here are some business benefits of blogging:

- Blogs help to position you and/or your company as experts and leaders in your industry.

- They're interactive by nature. At the end of each blog entry is usually a link that allows anyone to add their own comments to your blog entries. This allows your customers and potential customers to make comments about your products or services or ask you questions to help them in their buying process.

- Blogs are marketed easily and quickly by their RSS feeds.

- Blogs allow you to stress your choice of products, services, relevant news stories, quotes, pictures and more with your audience, customers and potential customers.

- People are generous with adding links to your blog if the content is good, especially within their own blogs. More links means more traffic and better search engine rankings.

Making money from your blog

Here are some ways you can make revenue from your blog:

1. **Selling advertisements**. Whether you use banners or text links, if your site draws a regular audience interested in your blog topics or theme, try to offer ad space to organizations that are looking to market to your audience. In

fact, if your blog becomes really popular then advertisers will call you.

2. **Offering Google's AdSense.** Google's website explains, "Google AdSense is a fast and easy way for website publishers of all sizes to display relevant Google ads on their website's content pages and earn money."

3. **Affiliate Programs.** Affiliate programs allow Websites who provide links to your site to receive payments or reciprocal advertising in exchange for promoting your Website. In the case of blogging, this is reversed. You post links within your blog, and collect money from the owners of those links when they result in a click-through and sale.

How to blog for business

The first step in blogging for business is to get blogging software. You can create a blog that is housed on another site such as http://www.blogger.com (a blog service) or you can host it on your own Web server. I recommend the latter since the links that are developed by others pointing to your blog won't be counted in the search engines because the links are attributed to domains. A link to http://MyNewBlog.blogger.com gives a link credit to blogger.com and not to your domain.

If your blog is a business blog, you ought to host your own blog as opposed to using a blog service. You need the extra functionality and control.

If you plan on hosting your own blog and if you plan to use a UNIX Web server platform, you need to go with blogging software such as Movable Type or WordPress, for example. If you have a Microsoft Web server platform for your site, you'll need software such as BetaParticle blog. At the following site you can find a great list of various blog software: http://www.lights.com/weblogs/tools.HTML

Next you'll need a database. The database stores the blog entries, among other things. If you don't know if you have a database on your website server or connected to it, or if you don't know how to hook up your blog to your database, contact your host company or Web server administrator for help.

Once you have the blog set up on your domain (for example http://www.MyWebsite.com/blog) and you've hooked it up to a live database, you can start blogging. Generally, each entry is also a day. So you can write a new entry every day, or whenever you want, and that entry will show up on the blog at the top, moving older entries below.

Think of a theme for your blog. It could be about your personal experiences in the industry you're in. It could be about your company's product reviews or new services. It could be about your thoughts and opinions about issues related to your industry. It could be a place where you regularly find and list new resources to help others in your industry. The list is endless. But be sure to stick to a theme and be original. You want to offer something of value to your website visitors.

Sticking to the theme helps you position yourself for future advertisers and makes for better reading by your visitors. You want to give a good impression with your blog with each entry if you want it to augment your online business. Finally, sticking to a theme helps the search engines find you since it's generally believed that engines determine website themes and use this information for ranking.

What's great is that blogs get indexed easily and quickly by search engines. Each entry is another "page" that may be listed in Google, for example, and will drive more traffic to your site.

Another neat thing about running a blog once it's set up is that you do not need to have any technical skills at all to make regular entries. This is helpful if you want to delegate the writing to someone else, since technical skills won't be a prerequisite. This allows you to have the most qualified person to share information related to the blog's theme and hopefully the best writer actually making the entries. If you want to learn more about blogging and business, look up the name Sherman Hu in Google and visit his sites; he offers a wealth of blogging knowledge.

Web 2.0

You've probably heard a lot of talk and excitement regarding the term *Web 2.0*.

Jack Humphrey (http://www.jackhumphrey.com/friday-trafficreport), a well-known Internet marketer who has truly embraced Web 2.0, defines it this way in his *Authority Black Book*:

> Generally speaking, if people can submit links to content, submit content, make comments and vote good/bad content up/down thus affecting the amount of traffic that content can generate, it's Web 2.0.

The name *Web 2.0* was most likely started by marketers. It explains a new generation of websites that take user-contributed content to a new level. The beginning of Web 2.0 consisted of simple forums that allowed people to join, post topics and reply to topics started by other members.

Now we have Web 2.0's more complex systems. Blogs, wikis, social bookmarking sites, and social networking sites are examples of Web 2.0 websites. Digg.com is an example of a Web-based service with members posting links to articles and other websites and other members voting on the articles. This helps still others decide what is best to read in a given category, and drives traffic to the articles with the highest vote.

Another example of a Web 2.0 site is the famed YouTube.com recently purchased by Google. YouTube also follows the Web 2.0 model with almost the whole site made up of users' submitted content, in this case digital video.

Yet another example of Web 2.0 websites is social bookmarking sites such as del.icio.us, which is an online version of your browser's "favorites" or "bookmarking" function. People join the site, post their bookmarks and make new bookmarks, and have the option of making their list public for others to see. Again, it's a Web 2.0 site because it's a community where members add content to the ever-growing site.

Squidoo is an example of an additional Web 2.0 site that allows members to create their own Web pages with whatever content they want. You don't need to be tech-savvy to use it.

Social networking sites such as Facebook and MySpace are Web 2.0 sites, too. These sites allow people to join and create their own Web page that represents them online. They can build a group of friends who link to their pages. People can leave comments, add photos and music and customize their pages.

Monetizing Web 2.0 sites has proven to be tricky, especially since a big selling point for these sites is that they're almost always free to join. Don't underestimate the power of a community that you manage, however. You could sell advertising and you could market to your e-mail list of the members, as long as you are judicious with the frequency and quality of your messages. Here's a list of some of the most popular Web 2.0 websites as of this writing:

http://www.squidoo.com
http://www.youtube.com
http://www.digg.com/
https://www.netscape.com
http://www.marktd.com/
http://www.plugim.com/
http://www.nowpublic.com/
http://slashdot.org/
http://reddit.com/
http://del.icio.us/
http://www.bibsonomy.org/
http://www.stumbleupon.com/
http://www.blinklist.com/
http://www.simpy.com/

Web 3.0

One last type of website, or more accurately, the Web in general, is something called Web 3.0. Wikipedia defines Web 3.0 as follows:

Web 3.0 is a term that is used to describe various evolutions of Web usage and interaction along several separate paths. These include transforming the Web into a database, a move towards making content accessible by multiple non-browser applications, the leveraging of artificial intelligence technologies, the Semantic Web, the Geospatial Web or the 3D Web.

In May 2006, Tim Berners-Lee was quoted in the *International Herald Tribune* stating that Web 3.0 is "a more revolutionary" Web. He said...

People keep asking what Web 3.0 is. I think maybe when you've got an overlay of scalable vector graphics— everything rippling and folding and looking misty on Web 2.0 and access to a semantic Web integrated across a huge space of data, you'll have access to an unbelievable data resource.

At the Seoul Digital Forum in May 2007, Eric Schmidt, CEO of Google, was asked to define Web 2.0 and Web 3.0. He responded:

Web 2.0 is a marketing term, and I think you've just invented Web 3.0. But if I were to guess what Web 3.0 is, I would tell you that it's a different way of building applications... My prediction would be that Web 3.0 will ultimately be seen as applications which are pieced together. There are a number of characteristics: the applications are relatively small, the data is in the cloud, the applications can run on any device, PC or mobile phone, the applications are fast and customizable. Furthermore, the applications are distributed virally: literally by social networks, by e-mail. You won't go to the store and purchase them...That's a very different application model than we've ever seen in computing.

In an article I wrote entitled "The Web of Tomorrow," I described my own vision for what the Internet will become,

20

which may be anywhere between Web 3.0 and Web 10.0. It includes a number of these key concepts. (Read it at http://www.oakwebworks.com/articles/future-web.htm).

Understanding Web 3.0 is probably not necessary for you, especially since there isn't even a consensus about what it is. Just beware that the rate of change and evolution on the Web, websites and Internet business as a whole, is fast paced. Understanding where the Web is headed will give you an edge on your competition by allowing you to adopt new technologies and paradigms that can successfully set you apart.

RSS Feeds

Another interesting way to put yourself ahead of the competition is through the use of RSS feeds. The official words making up the acronym RSS are Rich Site Summary, although it is also known as Really Simple Syndication.

In web terminology, "syndication" represents consolidating or summarizing content so that web users can not only publish updates to their websites but can also keep track of a large number of blogs or websites and load content into a location where they can read it at their leisure.

RSS is the variation (dialect) of the XML language (see the following paragraphs) that makes it possible for content on one website to be reposted (syndicated) by another. RSS feeds make it possible for you to let web users know what is new on your site. Enter "RSS feeds" in your favorite search engine to learn more.

What a Live Website Consists Of

Every website consists of a domain name, content and a host provider. To have a live website on the Internet, all three need to exist.

Today there are countless services that offer all of this in bundled packages. Yahoo, Earthlink, GoDaddy, Network Solutions, Register, Domain, HostGator and Domain Direct are just a few examples of companies that offer everything you need to get up and running. I recommend that you use these services to provide you with domain name and hosting services, but leave the content development and the website design and creation to someone you seek out and choose and a vendor you can work closely with.

If you choose instead to use bundled Web design services, you may be presented with a variety of website templates to choose from. The sites made from these are the trailer homes of the Internet. You don't get to craft your site to fit your specific business needs and goals; instead, you fit your business into these templates. More accurately, you crowbar your business into them and hope for the best but usually end up severely disappointed.

Don't go this route. Stay away from pre-fabricated website templates unless you don't mind numerous other websites out there that look exactly like yours.

If the Web design services that these companies offer refer you to a list of participating Web design companies, then you have a better chance of success. But you'll still need to correctly choose among the various vendors and work closely with that source throughout the entire process if you expect to have a successful final product.

To understand what makes up every website, let's look at its parts more closely.

Domain Names

An example of a domain name is *www.YourWebsite.com*. A domain name is unique and contains two parts, the actual unique name and the extension. A domain name is also called a URL (for Universal Resource Locator). In the above example, "YourWebsite" is the unique name and the ".com" is the extension. The .com extension is the most popular U.S. extension. Other examples of extensions are .net, .org, and .edu. Other countries use different extensions. Britain is .co.uk, Canada uses .ca, and Russia uses .ru, for example.

You buy domain names from registrars, basically domain name brokers. There are many registrars in existence today. My preference is to use the original company that used to have a monopoly on domain names back in the dawn of the Web, Network Solutions (http://www.networksolutions.com).

To determine if a domain name is taken or not (remember, they all have to be unique), go to Network Solutions and type in the name you are considering and you'll find out immediately if it's available.

An important thing to remember when buying and managing your domain name is that they are "rented" to you for a set period of years. This means they expire. So if you don't stay on top of it and renew, you risk someone else grabbing your domain name if you let it expire.

A Host Computer or Provider

The physical computer where the content of your website is stored is called a Web server. To access the content, you type in the domain name in an Internet-connected website, which then accesses the content stored on the computer that is physically located on a host computer and serves the content back to you. (This is basically the same process as opening up you're *My Documents* folder on a Windows machine and clicking on a file, except on the Web, the file is located on another computer.)

Simply put, if you want a new website you'll need a computer that's hooked to the Internet to store it. There are a huge number of host companies out there that will provide this service for you, often at very low prices. You can expect to pay a set-up fee and a monthly fee. The set-up fee is sometimes waived or could cost up to hundreds of dollars. And the monthly fee can range from a few dollars a month up to hundreds of dollars. Two popular hosting providers are GoDaddy.com and Earthlink.net.

Another option is to host your site yourself. This would mean having a computer at your place of work that you are totally in charge of. You would either have to learn a lot or hire someone who knows how to manage and administer a host computer, or server. for you. This may be the situation you already have set up if you are part of a larger business, but if you're a one-man band, it is far easier and more economical to utilize a host provider.

I recommend that you do a search for this to compare prices, features and services. But before you do this, you'll need to know what to choose from and how to compare.

Understanding where your website should live—your various hosting options—will allow you to make the right decision for your unique business situation and help you save time, money, and energy.

If you pay a monthly fee to have your site hosted by another company, there can be considerable savings with the right choice. Internet Service Providers (ISPs) provide people with access to the Internet. With this access, one can use the Web, which sits on top of the Internet infrastructure. Host companies are organizations that rent out space on their servers for individuals or organizations to keep their websites on. Sometimes host companies are ISPs as well.

What's important for a business owner or executive to know is that there are a number of choices when deciding where to physically locate the business website. Every website sits (or physically exists) on a server. Each server physically lives in one of two places. It may be located at its website owner's company, which is called in-house, internal, or self-hosting. For example, if a company has an active website and owns the server the website is on, and the server is physically located at their company, then it is self-hosting.

The other place a website server can physically live is at an ISP or Host Company, which is often called virtual hosting. This allows a company to avoid having to maintain its own Web server and connections to the Internet. There are a number of configurations the server can fall under in this category: dedicated server, co-location, or a shared server.

Each of these has advantages and disadvantages that need to be considered by decision makers. The following information illustrates some of the main differences among your hosting options:

In-House Server

- Company-owned, physically lives on site, on the company's premises

- You are in charge of all your support
- Buying and maintaining the machine is inexpensive, but time-consuming

Dedicated Server

- ISP/Host-owned computer that is used by only one company
- Support can be either the customer's or ISP/Host's responsibility
- You don't share the space, but you pay a setup fee, a monthly fee for both the computer and service, and pay for support

Co-located Server

- Customer/organization-owned computer
- Support is the customer's responsibility, in some instances the hardware will be supported by the ISP/Host
- You don't share the space, but you have to buy the computer, pay monthly fee, not pay for setup or support (must do it yourself)

Shared Server

- ISP/Host-owned computer that is used by more than one company at the same time
- Support is the ISP/Host's responsibility
- You share the space, rent the computer, pay a monthly service fee. Usually the least expensive option

Cost and support varies with the service. One of the first things a company's owner needs to understand is its resources. If the company has two employees and neither has any technical ability, then a co-located server may not be the best choice because they will be responsible for the technical setup, maintenance and troubleshooting of their website server. They may want to consider a shared server that provides all the setup and support for them and costs a lot less. In contrast, a multi-million dollar company may benefit most by a dedicated or co-located server where they have control over the machine but share some of the responsibility with the host company.

It may even be more advantageous for a large company to forgo outsourcing their hosting needs altogether and decide to host their websites in-house. This is practical only if there are employees skilled and available. If a business internally hosts its Web presence, they will need technicians to handle both the software and hardware of the server, networking people to deal with the connections to the Internet and security issues, and Web people (programmers, designers, and marketers) or people who have all these skills who create and maintain all the Web pages and services.

There are quite a few things to be considered when choosing a place to locate a company server. There are more hosting options than mentioned here, and more will emerge as time goes on, but understanding the basics will help your business save time, money and effort in the long run. If you decide to go with a shared server at a hosting company, be sure to research numerous potential companies. Services vary widely. Here are a few things you need to ask before you make any decision:

- Are there setup fees on top of monthly costs?

- Do you provide both software (operating system) and hardware support?

- Does your support service allow phone call inquiries or just e-mail inquiries?

- If just e-mail inquiries are allowed, how much does it cost to buy phone support?

- What kinds of programming languages (besides HTML) do you allow on your shared servers? For example, Java, CGI, Perl, ASP, etc.

- Will my site be on a UNIX or Microsoft server?

• Do you provide website server log file statistics? If so, do you offer a Web interface that I can use to view my website statistics or do I have to download the log files myself and run them in Webtrends or similar software?

Choosing the right place for your website to live is an important decision. Making the right one will definitely save you a large amount of time, energy and money.

The Content

Web content refers to all the files of text, images, applications and media that make up a Website. Web content can be static or dynamic. Static content doesn't change or move. Text and images in an HTML page are usually static. Dynamic content comes from a database and is processed the moment the user accesses it. (See Chapter 2, "Technology," for a complete description of dynamic content and databases). Media content can be audio or video files.

Dynamic content is managed by Web applications, code that runs on either the server or the client (see Chapter 2 – "Technology," for an explanation). Examples of website applications are forms that ask the user to give contact information that the user submits by clicking a button, or an e-commerce process where a user chooses a product and buys it with a credit card. There are many other types of interactive applications on the Web as well.

Creating Web applications is often more expensive than putting together a website consisting of simple text and images. If you want a website containing only static text and images, you should pay less than for a website that contains some sort of dynamic Web application. The higher cost comes from paying for a higher skill level for those who write code to create applications and more time needed to build them.

We'll get more in depth about content later.

How a Website's Content is Organized and Goes Live

Whether the website is made up of static content, dynamic content or a combination of both, fundamental building blocks are common to all websites.

Let's start with a simple example of a three-page static website. Our hypothetical website contains a Home Page, an About Us page and a Contact Us page. The home page is accessed on the Internet by typing the domain name (or URL) into your browser. When you arrive at the home page you'll see somewhere on the page two hyperlinks.

Links are generally blue and underlined and are the building blocks of websites and the Web as a whole. One link will say "About Us" and the other will say "Contact Us." When you click on each one you'll be brought to the corresponding Web page. On the home page, this list of two links is often called the navigation or "Nav bar."

Most sites have many pages organized under numerous sections. Navigation consists of a grouping of links that lead to each main section of the site.

In our three-page website, the site contains a total of three HTM or HTML pages (it can be either) that physically reside on a host computer, which is often called a server.

Before this site is live on the Internet you have to go to a domain name registrar (by going to their website or by calling them) to purchase an available domain name. You would have to have the three static Web pages created (a lot more on that later). Finally, you need to pay for a hosting service to provide a permanent place for the three pages to reside.

These three pages would sit on the host computer, or server, and await requests from people on the Internet typing in the corresponding domain name into their browsers.

Here are the steps involved in setting up your websites:

1. Buy a domain name from a registrar

2. Create Content

3. Pay for a hosting service

4. Hook the domain name up with the hosting service (associate the URL with the hosting service using DNS, which stands for Domain Name Server)

5. Move the content to the new host (FTP content to server. FTP stands for File Transfer Protocol)

That's it. After you accomplish these five steps, your site will be live and viewable from anywhere in the world where there is an Internet connection.

If you already have a website and are hiring a Web vendor to build a new website, most of this is probably already in place, and you'll be hiring a vendor only to create and organize new content and applications.

If you are starting from scratch, the Web vendor you hire should be able to do all of this for you. You should expect your Web vendor to take your idea and do everything it requires to transform that idea into a live website: find and buy a domain name, obtain a host provider, associate the domain name with the hosting provider's server assigned to you, and move the content they design and build onto the server.

Now that you understand what constitutes a real website, let's delve a little deeper to discover the three main disciplines that breathe life into websites. From my description above, you'll notice that the fundamentals that make up any website involve not only the content, but the way that content becomes viewable and usable on the Web.

The creation, organization and presentation of the content (design) and the electronically accessible characteristic of that content (technology) make up two of the three pillars of a every website. The third and final pillar of a successful website is its ability to be known to the outside world (marketing). Read on to gain an expert understanding of successful websites.

Chapter 2

Webbing Bells

The Marriage of Technology, Design and Marketing

In this chapter you'll learn about the three pillars or disciplines that make up every website. You'll also discover why every great website needs all three, and why your Web vendor needs to be well-versed in all three. The better you understand this, the better your final website will be.

By reading this section you'll know what to look for in other websites, what questions to ask when vetting potential Web vendors, what to request in each proposal submitted to you, and you'll have a superb understanding of what your final website ought to include.

The better you understand that a full-functioning and successful website is dependent upon these three pillars, the better your site will serve you for years to come.

In the highly disciplined art of karate, the *karate-ka*, or practitioner of karate, kneels while meditating. When done, the *karate-ka* will bow, placing his palms flat on the floor in front of him while having both thumbs touching and both index fingers touching. A triangle is formed in between his two hands. The three sides of this triangle represent mind, body and spirit.

In karate, these three elements are inseparable. To be successful, the *karate-ka* needs to develop all three continually. He will be ill-equipped to properly perform his art if he's missing one. Most importantly, when his life is being threatened by a thug in a dark alley and he has to call upon his karate training to defend himself, the degree to which he has trained and developed his mind, body and spirit will be the determining factor in his successful defense.

Tantamount to this, his ability to present a unified front that incorporates all three elements equally will decide his fate. To ignore even one of these essentials would be like a basketball team trying to win a game with fully developed passing and dribbling skills but with woefully deficient shooting abilities.

The Three Pillars of the Web

In the same way, the business owner or executive who is attempting to achieve a successful Web presence must incorporate three equally important elements: design, technology and marketing. These are the Three Pillars of the Web. The final product, the finished website, will suffer if any of these three elements is under-utilized or ignored.

Like the *karate-ka* who has trained his mind, body and spirit into a cohesive instrument to defend himself against an attacker, the business owner or executive must become knowledgeable in the fusion of Web design, Web technology and Web marketing to defend himself successfully in today's competitive business landscape.

The Web has become so integrated into business today that a successful Web presence is a necessity for survival.

When you decide you want a website you face the daunting task of deciphering the relationship among these three disciplines. You also need to learn how to incorporate proper design, marketing and technology into your Web presence whether you do it yourself or manage someone else while they do it. If you don't, you face lost revenues and, ultimately, extinction.

At the very least, you need to determine which people or organizations to turn to for help, understanding that the proper utilization of these three pillars can do more than anything else to elevate your presentation on the Web from the millions of other websites.

The pages that follow will provide a proper road map. Once you've learned how the pillars of the Web work together to make a great website, you'll know what your final product ought to look like. This will help you communicate to your Web vendor exactly what you're looking for.

Design and marketing tend to be right brain activities while technology and programming tend to be reserved for the left brain. Right or wrong, here are some general characteristics many people think of regarding designers, marketers and programmers. Designers can be creative, right brain thinkers who are visual and maybe even flamboyant.

Marketing is often practiced by extroverted people while programmers tend to be introverts. Marketers can be glitzy, showy, often embellishing and tweaking reality to match what they want to say to potential customers. Computer programmers can be a little nerdy, a lot black and white, and often don't say much.

In the past these disciplines haven't been required to overlap. From the arrival of the silicon chip, computing has been the realm of the geek, who wasn't expected to be socially adept. That's one of the reasons introverted people gravitate towards computer work. It involves dealing with people less than many other professions.

Universities don't generally offer classes that combine graphic design and computer programming. These disparate disciplines were relegated long ago to opposite sides of the campus, where they remain today.

This made sense in the past. Specialization is the domain of education. Artistic people took graphic design classes or went to art schools, and the techies took hardware and software classes and often went to engineering schools. These respective paths were followed after graduation when careers were made and developed.

People have a way of categorizing everything, including themselves. It's common for a woman to call herself a "left-brained thinker," a "people person," or an "artistic type." Why would an artsy graphic designer want to deal with a lot of 1s and 0s like programmers do? Why would a programmer care if something looked pretty or not? And why would an extroverted sales and marketing professional care about anything but making the sale?

Listening to a conversation between a graphic designer and a software programmer is like listening to a married couple in divorce court. They speak two different languages and have completely different needs and desires.

They often don't even use the same computers; designers use Macintosh Apples and programmers use PCs. Unfortunately, engineers sometimes look down on marketing departments and advertising people.

The reality is that designers, programmers, and marketers come from three different worlds. As we can see, the very ways in which we fundamentally think, communicate and learn are different, and by categorizing, specializing and separating things into neat little boxes, we have kept design, technology and marketing separated.

Then along came the Web. All of a sudden, there was an entity that had the potential to bridge the gap.

At first the Web was simply a way for computer people and scientists to use mostly technical skills in communicating and sharing information. There was no concern at the beginning for the way a document on the Web looked. Images weren't even part of the Web in the beginning; there was only text. In order to actually use the Web in the beginning, one needed to know how to make thorny modem connections to the Internet, and install complicated software that an average non-technical person would have had no hope in accomplishing.

Since at first people weren't trying to sell anything on the Web, marketing wasn't in the picture either. All this would change, and the disparate camps would be forced to spend a lot more time together, like a cat, dog and mouse trapped together on a boat, requiring a treaty to make their way ashore.

Once the free market started to seep into the Web, a need for design and marketing emerged. The Web's primary technical component no longer existed in a vacuum. As the need grew, the techies responded. Mark Andersen's Mosaic browser (later named Netscape) soon had the ability to display graphics, and in an instant graphic designers entered the fray.

By then the initial public offering of Netscape stock was catching the attention of capitalists. Within a short time, businesses everywhere began to toss up websites to represent their companies online in the hopes of staying with the pack and making more money. Indeed, the entire dot-com boom was started by capitalists and entrepreneurs developing online-only business models in anticipation of cashing in on the IPO frenzy.

And this is where the fundamental problem heated up. For the first time, people from different worlds started working together to create websites. It was a free-for-all, and in many respects, still is today. Programmers, networking administrators and hardware people had to work with graphic designers and marketers to create the finished product, the company website. The problem was that these people weren't used to dealing with each other so intimately.

Back in college, remember, they were on opposite sides of the campus or in different schools altogether. When they entered the working world, their cubes were on opposite sides of the office, on different floors, or even in another city.

Now these people were being tasked with creating what was becoming an integral part of their company's business, building a Web presence. The struggle was on and many web-sites offered a clear view of the disparity problem. From this scramble surfaced a clear need for a person who understood it all.

Enter the webmaster. This was a brand new job and quickly became a career for thousands of people. Filling the position was much easier than trying to define what a "webmas-ter" is. Being a webmaster could mean anything from being a Web designer to managing a Web server. It could represent someone whose job consists of posting content to the site of the person who runs the actual hardware where the company's web-site is located. It could describe the individual who designs the Web pages. Or it could mean any combination of these under-takings and more.

Today we are no closer to a clear definition. Executives who plan to downsize may love the idea of handing three jobs over to one person and calling that person a webmaster. In real-ity, the importance of a business's Web presence is so vital to the overall success of the business that one person assigned to fulfill all functions will face a real struggle trying to further the company's objectives with an online presence.

To get past this confusion, today we call a company that is supposed to make a website for us a Web Design Company. Since this is such a new field, names are not yet as accurate as they should be. A Web design company that you consider hiring ought to be much more than a design firm. It should be able to actually code and build your website and market it as well. If they can't do these things because they're just a design firm, be ready to shell out more money to another person or vendor to do the coding and marketing later.

It becomes clear that this entire area of Web development can be difficult to comprehend by a business owner or executive who needs to build or maintain a Web presence. Will a webmaster solve the problem? Should this person be the one who designs, builds and markets the site? Or will hiring a Web design company, a Web vendor, do the trick?

Whatever direction you choose, the business or individual building your site needs a firm grasp of each of the three Pillars of the Web. In this chapter, let's briefly look at each of the three disciplines that make up an effective Web presence.

Design

Web design is the process of creating a user experience arising from the look-and-feel, user interface and information architecture.

Basis of User Experience with WebSite		
look-and-feel (appearance)	User Interface (usability)	Information Architecture (organization)
Color schemes Font styles, sizes Font colors Graphics Page layouts	Links Forms Search capabilities	Site navigation Content organization Site maps

Figure 2.1

The most important factor in Web design is the user. The design of a website or Web service should be driven by the user's needs. One cannot practice Web design without being affected by the expectations of future users. A business website exists to communicate and help the user. Following this rule will help make sales.

The user needs to be central to the creation of a site. To ignore this principle would be like a retail store planner ignoring the fact that customers will soon be navigating through the store but insisting on creating a confusing floor plan that resembles a tortuous maze of racks, trapping even the most experienced person in a labyrinth of aisles of goods.

For success in accomplishing the goals of helping, communicating and selling to the user, a website must have an appropriate appearance and be intuitive to use.

A website's "look-and-feel" is a primary concern of Web design because the site's overall appearance consists of its color schemes, font styles and sizes, graphics, page layouts, and the way all these elements come together.

Beyond look-and-feel, Web design involves usability, the measure of a website's potential to accomplish the goals of the user. It is achieved with a tool we call the User Interface, the ways a user can interact with the site and the ways that the site invites interaction and responds to it. Other types of user interface (UI) include HTML forms and site search functions. Any element of a Web page that invites user interaction can be considered part of the UI.

For example, hyperlinks in the form of text or buttons are a type of user interface because they make it possible for a site visitor to move among the site's pages and respond to the site. The user has to interact with the links by clicking on them to get the desired result of visiting another page.

The easier it is for a visitor to use a site's navigational system, the better its usability. If a website contains ten main sections, and each section has a different set of navigation links located in different spots in each section, this site's usability is rather low. With a setup like this, each time a site user enters a new section, extra time is needed to hunt for the navigational links and figure out a new navigational system. Making the user work too hard can turn off many people.

Because leaving your website is as simple as clicking a mouse, frustrated users won't stick around. Within seconds the user is enjoying a site that is far more intuitive.

If you've ever been lost in a large retail store or struggled to find what you were looking for, you know how frustrating wandering around helplessly can be. It is even worse online. At least in a brick and mortar store, you have a frame of reference. You can see where the walls are and can usually see an "exit" sign that you can follow.

Websites can give a feeling of being lost in space because there are fewer visual cues to give the visitor reference. Good Web design consistently tells the visitor exactly where they are. There's a logo in the top left of the page, a page title, bread crumb links at the top, a clearly defined Home link to let them start over, a consistent look-and-feel and navigation across all pages.

Another aspect of usability is the site's information architecture, the way all the content and information on the site is organized. If the organization doesn't make sense, the site isn't very usable. Therefore, the way in which all the information on the site is structured plays a vital role in the usefulness of the site and should be determined in the design. A site's navigation system is a perfect example of Web information architecture. See Chapter 7 and Chapter 8 to learn more about creating effective website navigation systems.

Picture a loose-leaf corporate binder with fifty independent laminated pages, each representing a piece of vital company information. Every page's look-and-feel—colors, fonts, and images—is beautiful. Unfortunately, the fifty pages are thrown into the binder haphazardly, with no forethought of organization or relationships. If you had to learn one specific piece of information about the company that you thought may be found in the binder, you'd have to sift through every page until you found what you were looking for.

A table of contents and numbering each page would help. Organizing the pages by sections, where each section contained related pages, would make it even easier to use.

In Web design, each Web page can be likened to one loose leaf binder page, the navigation system is a kind of table of contents, and the way the entire site's pages, information and content are organized is its information architecture. Since hyperlinks form a site's navigation system and is therefore the way a user views and interacts with the content on the site, navigation links and information architecture are closely related. The effectiveness and harmony of look-and-feel, usability and information architecture form the basis for solid Web design.

In site design, the number one question to be asking is, "How can I design our site's appearance and usability to optimally achieve our business's goals?"

Beware of design for design's sake. This applies to all aspects of building a website. When carrying out any action involving your business's website, from designing to coding, to maintaining and marketing, the issue of optimizing achievement of your business's goals and facilitating the user's experience should be front and center at all times.

Web design does not exist in a vacuum. Usability is not only a part of design, but is also an integral part of Web technology. When a pure traditional designer who has no technical background creates a mock-up of a desired future Web page, inherent issues will almost always be encountered by the programmer. Like it or not, the design of a website will be forever married to Web technology.

Technology

Web technology varies in depth and changes all the time. One could spend a lifetime learning about it, and never fully know it all because of its constantly changing nature. This section will explore the Web's core principles that are necessary for a business owner or executive to understand in order to create and maintain an effective website.

Since this book is for the non-technical business person, I am going to explain some basic technical concepts that will help you grasp the fundamentals of the technical side of the Web. Armed with just this small amount of technical knowledge, you won't get bamboozled by unscrupulous Web programmers.

Just as in Web design, the most important facet of Web technology is the user. Web design and Web technology are truly inseparable. Creating and then utilizing even a simple Web banner involves more than just design. It also involves technical knowledge. More importantly, it involves understanding user needs. The first steps of creating and utilizing a Web banner may involve pure design. A designer produces a design concept of how the banner should look. Once the banner's appearance is created, technical issues immediately emerge.

To understand the related technical issues, we need a brief description of how Web files and sizes work on the Web. A Web page is the same as any other file on a computer. The rules that apply to a Microsoft Word document also apply to a Web page. Every computer file has a specific "weight" that is determined by the elements in the file. If a document has one paragraph of text in it, then it will "weigh" less than a document that has 100 paragraphs of text in it. The larger the file, the more computer resources are required to store and present it. The higher the level of resources needed, the lower the performance. Images and rich media such as audio or video files weigh much more than text. In a Web page file, text, images, and rich media all add to the page's weight.

So a Web page, which again is really just a computer file, varies in weight depending on the amount of text, images, and other media in it. Since larger amounts of these elements require more computer resources to store and present it, performance is affected. We measure performance in Web terms by how long a page takes to appear in a user's browser after the user clicks the link to view it. This is called page loading time.

The system of connections (or pipes) in the Internet which deliver content from a server computer to a client's computer browser is made up of fiber optic cables, telephone wires and other transfer devices. Their size is finite. This means that the larger the amount of data that needs to be transferred, the slower the rate of transfer will be.

Let's go back to our banner example. If the banner image is "heavy," it will take longer to transfer it from the server where it physically exists to a user's client computer. If an image is intricate, large and has many colors, it may be a beautiful image, but it will weigh a lot. Thus, it will travel slowly through the Internet's pipes, causing the Web page to take longer to load.

As you can see, we need a balance between the design and weight of the banner. On one hand is the issue of pure design, how aesthetically pleasing the banner is, and on the other is pure technology—how much the banner weighs. Throughout Web development, there is a constant interplay between design and technology. Let's examine in a little more detail what Web technology is and what it's made up of.

Web technology is the infrastructure, hardware and software that brings the Web to life. It is the mechanism that allows one person to publish Web content to a server and another person across the globe to view that content on their own computer.

Many processes going on "under the hood" make this all possible. It is beneficial to break down the abstract concept of Web technology into four subsections: client/server model, hosting, processes and functionality, and databases.

Client/server model: The client/server model deals with the relationship between two computers or two programs in which the client makes a service request from the server, which fulfills the request. Most often, the client program is physically located on one computer and the server program is located on another computer. In a network, which is two or more connected computers, the client/server model provides a way to interconnect programs that are distributed across different locations. The Internet is a network of networks, or a super network, and utilizes the client/server model.

In the Internet, the browser on a personal computer is called the client. Microsoft's Internet Explorer is an example of a browser. A server is another computer that has Web pages on it and software that enables it to wait for and respond to client requests. Think of the client/server model like a restaurant patron and waitress. The waitress has access to all the meals prepared in one place, the kitchen. When a patron asks for a particular meal, the waitress goes to the kitchen and retrieves it for the patron. She can retrieve and deliver the same meal for any number of customers, or she can give different meals to different people, depending on their requests.

Two important fundamental protocols associated with the Web are HTTP (Hypertext Transport Protocol) and TCP/IP (Transmission Control Protocol/Internet Protocol).

HTTP is the set of rules for transferring files (text, graphic images, sound, video, and other multimedia files) on the Web. HTTP is like the specific rules our waitress has to follow in order to properly retrieve and deliver the correct meals. TCP/IP is the communication language of the Internet, like English for the waitress. All Web clients and servers have TCP/IP software loaded and operating on them.

Why is all this important for a business owner to know? First, these are fundamental concepts of the Web, and understanding these fundamentals will give the business owner an advantage in the effective utilization of the Web. More importantly, vital technological decisions need to be made that directly affect an organization's bottom line. Customers use varying clients (computer platforms and browsers) and are therefore presented with differing versions of the same website. Different clients render the same website in different ways, and it's important for a business to understand exactly how their Web presence is being viewed.

For example, if a company's main customer uses Macintosh computers with a Firefox browser and their website is developed and tested only for PCs using Internet Explorer, the site the customer sees could be radically different from the site the company intended to display.

Every website needs a physical place to reside, a server. A business has many choices here. Servers come in all flavors and styles, and one kind will be beneficial and advantageous for one company but a liability for another. A business owner or executive who has a stake in the business's Web presence must be educated in this as well in order to make the proper business decisions.

Let's look at another important aspect of Web technology, hosting.

Hosting: Internet Service Providers (Asps) provide people with access to the Internet. With this access, one can use the Web, which sits on top of the Internet infrastructure. Host companies are organizations that rent out space on their servers for individuals or organizations to park their websites. Sometimes host companies are Asps as well.

(Refer back to "A Host Computer or Provider" in Chapter 1 for an in-depth look at hosting.)

Be sure to ask the person or company who is building your site where the site will be hosted.

Processes and functionality: One thing that makes the Web so awesome is its ability to allow users to interact with it. A website gives a customer an active role in learning about or buying a product or service. Unlike television or magazine articles, a customer doesn't passively view a website. Links can be clicked, forms can be filled out, information can be searched, and customized products or services can be created. And the potential goes well beyond this. As Web technology becomes increasingly sophisticated, interactive capabilities grow.

Another aspect of Web technology is the functionality it provides the user. Basic Web pages are created using HTML (hypertext markup language), the language used to print content to a Web page. HTML is used to render a Web page and gives the website creator the ability to embed text, graphics and multimedia files into a page.

That is just the beginning. To make the page interactive and give it functionality beyond hypertext clicking, other programming languages are needed.

An example of website interactivity requiring more advanced functionality is the online form. More often than not, a website contains one or more forms that ask the user to enter personal information and submit the completed form back to company. This allows users to interact with the company, giving them the ability to speak directly to the organization. In turn, it allows the company to learn more about their existing or potential customers.

Much goes on behind the scenes to make a form actually work. First there is the HTML that allows the appearance of the form in the Web page to exist. Then there is code beyond HTML that goes into action when the user clicks the "submit" button at the end of the form. Many programming languages can be used to accomplish this. Their selection depends on the software and hardware (or platform) of the company's server as well as the skills of the people coding the website and form.

When considering possible Web design companies (Web vendors) to build you a new site or re-vamp an existing one, be sure to ask what technologies they regularly use to add functionality to their clients' sites. Ask them if they have programmers on staff and what languages they know. They would need to know more than just HTML if they are going to be able to build you forms, dynamic pages and interactive features. Typical Web programming languages are PHP, Java (and Java Server Pages) and ASP or ASP.Net. The person or company you hire ought to know and be able to use one of these languages or ones like them.

Companies can benefit only by making the effort to explore how the Web's inherent potential to engage the customer can increase the value of the website and thus increase revenue to the business. An HTML form is only the beginning. It is particularly helpful for organizations to look at their offline processes and try to recreate them online in a manner that is appropriate to the Web. When this is accomplished, time, money and resources can be saved.

For example, the prices a company posts on their website may need to be updated regularly. The more products are displayed and the more often prices are changed, the more money a business can save by putting all the prices in a database and making the website database driven dynamically to pull the pricing out of the database in real time so the pricing on the site is always current. Otherwise they may end up spending too much precious time answering telephone calls from customers or partners who want to know the most current prices.

Automating price changes saves time, money, and other resources. Without this tool, if a certain price is listed in a number of areas on a site, the business has to pay someone to make the update in each place every time the price changes. They also have to pay people to answer telephone calls regarding price changes. Maybe the pricing stays the same most of the time, but what about when a business runs specials and discounts?

Another benefit is that the entire company can refer to the website to get the most updated pricing. Let's say a business runs a special and reduces the price of a product. Do all the sales people need to be contacted and educated about the discount? By making this a website function, the company would simply change one entry in their database and refer everyone to the Web to get the current price. Any company information that regularly changes can be automated using the Web.

Of course to accomplish the migration from offline to online services, knowledge and skills in Web technology are required. By understanding business Web needs, proper choices can be made in purchasing hardware or software and in hiring the people best suited for the tasks.

We've already discussed functionality and usability in the scope of Web design. Again, it becomes clear that technology and design go hand in hand. If a database-driven pricing service on the Web is not designed properly from the start, its usability may be poor and defeat the purpose of saving time, money and resources. If customers can't use it easily, then in their frustration they may telephone your business even more often than before to get clarification. Or they may choose another source for the products or services you are offering. In our pricing Web service example, a key component was the database. The database is an extremely important component of the Web and deserves its own discussion.

Databases: Our exploration of Web technology has led us to the database, a basic building block of the Web. Although it may not be apparent when we're surfing the Web, many sites are driven by databases of all kinds. What is a database?

In its simplest form, a database is a collection of information organized so that it can easily be manipulated. Databases are based on software packages that facilitate the access, management, and updating of related information. Many software database packages exist, with new ones being released often. Each has a unique way of allowing information to be manipulated. The set of tasks offered by databases will often determine which package is best.

Databases vary as much in cost as they do in functionality. Some are free and others cost tens of thousands of dollars. It is important to determine exactly what database needs exist, if any, before deciding on a database package. This will help guide you in how much to spend on it.

The database and the Web is a match made in heaven. One of the tenants of the Web is the dissemination and sharing of information. What better way is there to store and manipulate data and information than in a database? Databases have been in existence for a lot longer than the Web, but once the Web was developed, people quickly realized that organizing information was a priority.

Tim Burners-Lee was motivated to create the Web because he wanted a way for scientists at CERN to be able to share their data stored in databases in a standardized and easy way.

The process of getting data from an organization's database onto the Web for all to view is again a question of Web technology.

Here's how it works. The company has a database package with data already in it. This database may sit on the company's Web server, or it may be on its own dedicated machine. Either way, the database software is connected to the server which allows its data to be accessed. When a user gets on the Web and views that company's website, he uses his browser to make a request. Or he may "call" the company's server that houses the website.

Let's say that you want to view information located inside the database. First, the website and server must be configured to allow this and carry it out. The user's browser makes a request to the website server. This triggers the server to make a request to the database. The database searches for and then retrieves the requested data, sends it to the server which in turn sends it to the client (the user's browser) where he then is able to view it. See Figure 2.4.

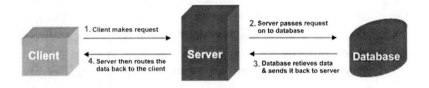

Figure 2.4

Databases can improve the functionality of a website in several ways. For example, let's suppose that the data a user enters into a Web form are sent to and stored in a database. Later, when the user goes back to that site, mechanisms are available matching the user's preferences and are embedded within the Web pages that can be viewed by the user. This customizing can be a valuable service for a customer.

Often when a company has a large number of products, every product and its associated information is stored in a database. This allows a user to easily view any product they wish.

Search engines employ databases as well. When you type in a keyword in a search engine, you are initiating a search in the search engine's databases. The appropriate websites are then served back to the user. A huge range of uses exist today for databases on the Web, and more are being created regularly.

A number of issues have plagued Web technology. One is the constant change and innovation in protocols and methods for accomplishing Web-related tasks. Another issue is the attempt at transforming pre-Internet technology into Web technology. With that effort, a significant number of antiquated technologies have been altered to fit today's Net, and in the process the Web has suffered. A perfect example of this is the use of telephone lines to transmit Internet data. The old copper wires originally developed for voice only have been widely adopted to transfer data over the Net using dial-up connections. But they are extremely limited and cause Web pages to load slowly. Fortunately, more efficient ways of transferring data are now used such as cable and fiber optics and this will improve.

Even with new challenges every day, Web technology is in a constant state of enhancement. Enriched and innovative Web technology continues to make people's lives easier and improve global communication.

You and your business are not able to harness the power of the Web until you have an understanding of the workings, advantages and disadvantages of various Web technologies that affect your business. The best possible use of Web technology will not benefit a company at all unless potential customers are aware of the site's existence. A beautifully designed and robustly interactive and functional website does a company little good if no one visits it. And that is why Web marketing is the third essential Web element.

Web Marketing

Imagine building and opening a new store in a relaxing, rural farmland area someone almost never wanders past. Now imagine that this new store has the best new products in the world. It has a state-of-the art facility for shopping and enjoyment. The store is wonderful to be in, aesthetically pleasing and the employees are a delight to deal with. Huge sums of money are spent on every facet of the business—except promotion. And no one came.

Why would they? How could they have known the new store even existed?

It's the same on the Web. In fact, the Web is a more rural and desolate place than anywhere else on Earth, and yet Web marketing is the lifeblood of a company's e-business. Web marketing, or e-marketing, is as fluid as Web technology. It is constantly changing. What works today may not work as well tomorrow. But if you want your business to succeed in an Internet-driven business world, you must be willing and able to market your website regularly.

See Chapter 9 ("After it's built, you HAVE to market it") for a detailed description of some of the top Web marketing techniques used today. Expect every technique you learn about to change and evolve.

The main goal of commerce is to produce revenue. The essence of e-marketing is driving traffic to a website and converting visitors into customers to increase sales. It is not only vital to drive traffic, but also to direct qualified traffic to a positive decision to buy.

The prerequisite to successful e-marketing is proper Web design and programming. This is why designing, constructing and coding a website needs to be done with the end user in mind at all times.

Since your website's goal is to bring as many qualified people to it as possible, your site must be designed for the user, or the user will leave immediately. It is too easy for someone to click to another site. People will look for any excuse to leave. They have little patience and high expectations.

If your business invests time and money and succeeds in attracting visitors to your website, the next challenge is to have a site that is good enough to keep the visitors there. Another term for this is "stickiness." The stickier a site, the longer visitors stay there. (See Chapter 7's "Great Website Qualities" list to learn more about this.)

The sole purpose of designing, creating, coding and maintaining a company website is to attract visitors, promote the business and make more sales. The proper marriage of design, technology and marketing will produce revenue.

A website can be accessed by ten people or ten thousand and it won't affect the site (as long as the proper Web technology is in place to handle the load). So the more qualified people that go to a site, the better, and it will not necessarily require any more Web resources. Once a site is built, every effort needs to be made to continually drive qualified people to the site.

Many different ways are available to drive qualified traffic to a site. Although the marketing methods are constantly changing, the principles stay the same. If the fundamentals can be understood and applied in new and creative ways, a business can continue to attract people regardless of changes that occur. Some of these principles are taken right from traditional advertising and marketing. Others are unique to the Web. Here are the main ones to understand.

E-Marketing Principles: Never forget the basic principles of drawing visitors to your site and building loyalty to your business because of what they learn from you. Here they are:

- People need to be given a reason to visit a site.

- People don't care about you, your business or your website; they only care about what your business, through your website, can do for them.

- People won't give you anything for nothing in return. If you ask them for their personal information, for example, be prepared to give them something in return. This is called an incentive.

- People are motivated first by emotion.

- One-to-one marketing is a reality on the Web.

- The Web is interactive by nature. Therefore it's easy to ask your visitors what they think, what their needs are and what you want to know about them. This in turn allows you to respond to their needs more accurately.

- An e-marketing program is always dynamic. As the data comes in about the success or failure of the program, adjustments need to be made for continual improvement.

- The Web offers immediate and exact feedback about e-marketing initiatives' success. Take advantage by analyzing the data constantly. Use server Web log files and website analytics programs (such as Google Analytics or WebTrends) to help you analyze your website's activity.

- Driving traffic to a site is often not enough; the traffic needs to be converted into paying customers.

- People crave useful, free and relevant information online. Give it to them and they will be more loyal to you.

- The less you tout your company, product or service in the useful information you're offering your website visitors (or e-mail list), the more people will trust you and be loyal to you.

Many of these principles can be applied using e-mail and website forms. For instance, one-on-one marketing can be realized by establishing a dialog with site visitors by first asking them to fill out a form where they give their e-mail address, and then periodically sending them e-mails tailored to their specific needs. You are much more likely to obtain a site visitor's e-mail address if you offer them something in return, known as an incentive.

This is illustrated by e-newsletter signups on home pages. Some website home pages contain a text field asking for a user's e-mail address, and in return promise a periodic e-newsletter sent directly to the visitor's in box. The visitor will sign up only if he believes that the newsletter has some value, such as information relevant to his career or hobby. If he believes the newsletter has no value because it's just another advertisement, then he will not give his e-mail address. His primary concern is what the newsletter can do for him.

This dynamic and interactive nature of the Web facilitates open dialog with visitors, allowing companies to ask specific questions about individual preferences. After a company acquires this information, it can be used to better market to the individual. This was much more difficult before the Web.

Website forms, news groups, Web 2.0, e-mails and online forums are all examples of ways in which customers can directly communicate with companies. Companies can now ask everything they ever wanted to know about existing customers so they can continue to effectively sell to them. And company websites, through the use of these features, can ask potential customers what they need and want, which will give them extremely useful information to help them sell more.

Another vital aspect to understand and apply in e-marketing is the Web's ability to provide immediate feedback regarding user activity. In traditional marketing and advertising, determining exactly how many people actually took action as a direct result of a print advertisement, for example, was extremely difficult. But advertising on the Web can be tracked accurately. By analyzing server log files, a company can determine how many users visited the site as a result of a specific banner advertisement or pay-per-click campaign.

E-mail marketing provides exact statistics as well. Within hours after an e-mail goes out to a list, a company can determine how many people visited the site as a result of reading the e-mail, and how many people purchased the product or service. The amount of statistical data is endless. All e-marketing campaigns can be perfectly analyzed. This allows immediate adjustments to be made, thereby providing the ability to constantly improve the initiatives.

Chapter 9 goes into more detail about utilizing all these e-marketing principles. I will explain exactly how to use each of these to produce revenue.

One of the most important points to grasp about the Web is that *content is king*. Content can be articles, white papers, opinions, instructions, videos or audio files. The more high-quality content you provide your site visitors, the more sales you'll eventually make. The content not only needs to be of high quality; it also needs to be relevant, fresh, generic—and free. In other words, the content needs to be relevant to your industry, updated and added to, free of charge and not advertise your company, products or services.

If people think you're just hawking your goods through your content, it won't be well received. If they feel that you're offering them constant new content that's fresh, free, relevant and that doesn't tout your products, they'll keep coming back to your site for more. You'll begin to establish a reputation as an authority in your industry. These two factors will eventually increase your sales. As a bonus, search engines love new content. So by constantly adding new content to your site, you're increasing your visibility to the search engines, thereby increasing your chances of being found by new people.

It's impossible to conduct just about any e-marketing initiative without the existence of a website and a technological infrastructure. This is essential to understand. If a company has no website, qualified traffic has nowhere to go. Furthermore, if a website exists containing only text and images, there is no way for a site visitor to interact with the company besides sending an e-mail. In other words, to fully utilize and take advantage of most e-marketing initiatives, there needs to be underlying Web technology to support it.

Even a simple e-mail campaign needs Web technology support. Many companies have acquired e-mail addresses of their customers. When a company is about to release a new product, it would be beneficial to send an e-mail to all the addresses announcing the upcoming new product release.

Often existing customers are receptive to new products or services, so an e-mail has the potential to generate revenue. But what happens when a customer receives the e-mail announcement, is interested, but has to wait until the product release date to purchase it? Should the company hope that the customer marks down the release date in their calendar? Expectations based only on hope often occur in traditional marketing.

The Web allows much more precise and dependable action—but only if the technology is there to provide it. Instead of hoping the customers have a good memory, the e-mail could ask the customer to click through to a form that sits on their company website. That form could ask the user if they want to be notified the day the product is released. Then, it becomes the company's responsibility to follow up. Creating Web forms, e-mail notifications, and databases to hold customer information is the realm of Web technology. It should be clear to you that if you want to take advantage of all the benefits of e-marketing, an infrastructure needs to be in place.

As the business owner or executive, you do not necessarily need to know how to create a Web form or database, but you do need to know that such things are needed in many e-marketing initiatives. You need to know that your website is designed properly, is easy to use and its information is organized in a user-friendly manner. You need to know specific Web marketing techniques that can be employed. And finally, you need to know that in order to employ these techniques an infrastructure needs to be in place. Whether you tackle this by yourself or hire a Web vendor to do it, it is vital to know that these three interrelated Web elements exist and how they are connected.

In conclusion, the three pillars of any great website are design, technology and marketing. Design encompasses usability, look-and-feel and information architecture. Technology includes where a website is hosted, how it functions and what code makes it work. Marketing involves various initiatives to attract website visitors and make them customers.

All three pillars need to be present for a website to have a chance at being great, serving your visitors and meeting your goals. The better you understand this, the better equipped you're going to be to hire the right Web vendor for you. Finally, once you have your website up and running, understanding these concepts, especially the marketing techniques, will allow you to get as much out of your site as possible.

You may be thinking about hiring a graphic designer. Before you do so, determine if the person has technical and marketing expertise. If you're considering hiring someone who is a technical computer whiz, verify that the person has skills in design and online marketing. Don't sell your business short by hiring only a third of what you need. Be sure your workers have the skills you need in all three of these disciplines. Section 2 will explain how to find just such a Web vendor.

SECTION 2

HOW TO HIRE A WEB DESIGNER OR WEB DESIGN COMPANY

Here's a personal story to help get you prepared for hiring a Web vendor.

My wife and I wanted to finish our basement and decided to hire a contractor. After a little research and a few quick conversations with a couple of friends we started to realize what a mine field we were about to navigate. Apparently hiring building and construction contractors is a tricky business that could leave you broke and your house in shambles.

We did a tiny bit of research online and found a website that listed local contractors who were licensed in our state. We called four of them and three called us back. We made separate times for each of the three to come to our house, assess the basement project and give us a time line and a price. We did not take any more time in learning what the project entailed.

The first contractor was a big man with an accent who came with an even bigger man who had an even thicker accent. They immediately made me uncomfortable. My first thought was, "Do I really want these two guys in my house for a month?" Since my wife and I know next to nothing about construction or basement finishing (and didn't bother to learn in advance) we asked these two fellows a number of questions. Half our questions were met with laughter, like we were two idiots.

I imagine that if I had taken the time to learn more about basement finishing we would have avoided looking ignorant. And I guess in the world of contractors, we were rather dumb. They came back with a price that was painfully high and not itemized. They said it would take about three weeks to finish. Strike one.

I suspect that since we asked questions that clearly revealed our ignorance, they felt comfortable charging us the highest price possible.

The second contractor showed up and told us right off the bat that he had a full time job and just did contracting on the side. He said it would take at least a month and maybe even two months. He seemed nice but never got back to us with a price quote. Strike two.

The third contractor seemed particularly affable. He talked about what he would do, how he would do it and was very personable, asking questions about our house and how long we lived there for and why we wanted the basement finished. We liked him immediately. He said if we wanted the floor of the basement done, it would take him two weeks, if not then it would take only one week. We thought we had found our guy.

He came back with a price that was just about the exact same as the first two guys and it was not itemized either. Although the price seemed high, what did we know? And it seemed to match the price for basement-finishing systems that we saw advertised on TV.

Then our water heater broke, and I ended up hiring my cousin, who is a professional plumber. While fixing it I showed him the contract for the basement finishing project that the third contractor had sent us. My plumber cousin is an expert in dealing with contractors; he owns several houses and properties and hires them all the time.

He laughed and proceeded to tell me all about how one needs to be very careful with contractors. First, he said we were almost definitely being price-gouged. He asked why the pricing wasn't itemized. He asked why the contract didn't have a project end date specified. He asked why the contract made no mention of sub-contractors, when more often than not there are sub-contractors involved. He asked what kind of materials were going to be used and why they weren't specified better in the contract. He asked why there were no contingency plans in place in case the contractor encountered a problem. He went on and on. The more he talked, the more foolish I felt.

So I called our chosen contractor up and asked him all the questions my cousin had just asked me. He basically refused to give any more details. He didn't want to give a project end date in the contract "in case things came up." My cousin had warned me that often contractors will get towards the end of the job and land another job they have to start somewhere else. If this happens, then they can drag out the last ten percent of your project because they're splitting their time between two jobs.

This contractor not only refused to give an end date; he also refused to itemize the services (which made me believe he padded the entire thing), and he refused to guarantee that if something came up that he didn't foresee, he wouldn't charge us extra. In other words, even if we never asked him to do anything else after we signed the contract and he was in the middle if the project, he could at any time say that he ran into a snag and could charge us more than what we originally agreed.

So we ended up not hiring him. There are obviously differences between contractors and Web vendors, but keep this story in mind when you are about to hire any vendor for anything. Do your homework. Be sure to have a grasp of what the project will entail. Speak to people who have been through it before. Know your top price based on what is reasonable within the industry and demand a definite project completion date. The more you know in advance, the more likely your project will end in success. That's why you're reading this book.

Chapter 3

Start with the End in Mind

Answer Four Questions and Create a Rough Outline

One key concept that many would-be entrepreneurs and business people miss is understanding market needs in advance. In other words, many people make the mistake of developing a product or service before they know if there is a need for it in the marketplace. This can be extended to websites as well.

Since a website is an extension of your business, and in many cases the only representation of your business, be sure you know there is a need for your business before you invest time and money building one. If you're re-vamping an existing site, be sure you understand in advance what the new site ought to have to better serve your market. Don't build a website before you nail down exactly what you want it to do for you in advance. What is its purpose and how is it going to help you achieve your business goals?

There are four main questions you need to answer before you begin your search for a Web vendor to do website creation for you. If you're not armed with the answers to these questions in advance, you're going to waste your time and money, experience unneeded grief and possibly risk creating a complete dud.

I recommend that you create a document that has the answers to these questions in it, along with a rough outline of the features you want to include in your website. I'm going to call this your Website Plan Document.

Website Plan Document

By having your Website Plan Document in hand at the onset of your search, you'll be able to narrow down the field of possible Web vendors to hire and you'll have something to give your prospective vendors to help them come up with an accurate proposal and an itemized price quote.

Another reason this is important to do is that without it you'll end up having to pay the Web vendor you choose to create this document as part of the proposal, so you'll save money by doing it yourself. I'll explain how to create this rough outline at the end of this chapter.

Here are the first two questions I ask any potential client when they seek out my business to help them build a website:

- What will be the site's goals and purpose?

- Who will be your website's audience?

These are the two most important questions you need to answer before you do anything else. The last two questions are also important to determine in advance:

- What is your budget?

- What is your timeframe?

Let's look more closely at these questions.

Question 1: What will be the site's goals and main purpose?

The first item to write down in your Website Plan Document is your site's goals and purpose. If you're hiring a Web vendor (a freelancer or firm) to build your own new website or if you've been tasked by a superior to hire someone to build one or revamp an existing one, here are the questions you need to answer:

1. Why do we need a website?

2. What are the ways in which this website is going to make us more money?

3. How will it make our business run better, faster and/or more cheaply?

4. What are the results we expect to get out of it?

Don't build a website "because everyone else has one." Don't build a website because all your competitors have one. Don't build a website to stroke your ego. Build a website to increase your business's bottom line, to streamline your supply chain, to reach a wider audience, or to offer a new way to communicate with your customers and prospects.

Here are a few things your website could do for you (this is not a complete list):

- Build your brand, get your name out

- Help you sell products directly over the Internet.

- Provide product information to drive local sales

- Automate repetitive tasks that waste your or your employees' time

- Provide educational information

- Allow you to sell advertising

- Help you build a community

- Help build a prospect list to which you can then market

- Help you resell someone else's products or earn affiliate commissions

- Facilitate getting your message out

- Any combination of the above

The sooner you determine your site's main purpose for existence, the easier it will be to determine what you need and don't need. This in turn will help you describe your needs to the Web vendor you choose, so that the work will take less time and effort and therefore cost you less.

Web developers, designers and firms offer different skill sets and specialize in different areas. The clearer the picture you have of what you want, the easier it will be to choose the service provider that fits your needs.

For example, if all you want to do is communicate with your customers, then maybe a business blog would fit your needs the best. You would seek a Web designer who specializes in blog building. Or you may want to sell products online and be able to manage all the Web content in-house. In that case, an e-commerce site with a back-end Web-based content management system would be in order, and you may need a larger Web firm to handle the programming and development.

Or maybe you are a solo entrepreneur who wants to start selling your e-books online. Then you may require a small, static website that has a few nicely designed pages and links to download your e-books and links to a third-party payment system like Paypal.

I suggest you write down exactly what you want to accomplish with your website in your Website Plan Document. Write down what you hope it will do for you on a daily, monthly and yearly basis. Describe what your ideal site would be, how it will make your life and other people's lives easier and how it will make you money.

The last part of answering this question involves trying to determine in advance the elements of your future website. Will it be a static site with no interactivity? If so, how many different sections do you think it needs and roughly how many pages of content do you imagine? Will you require your site to have functionality such as processing credit cards or form capabilities so you can ask for customer information that is sent to a database?

You may not know the exact answers to these questions, and may want the input of an experienced website designer/builder to help you, but the more you know now, the better off you're going to be. At least try to come up with a rough estimate.

Question 2: Who will be the website's audience?

The second vital question to answer and record in your new Website Plan Document helps you focus on your primary market. It may seem like an obvious step, but you'd be surprised how many people miss it. The Web is the greatest marketing medium ever invented and is far more than just another marketing medium.

Marketing is all about your audience and message. Your audience is made up of people who will be most likely to visit your website—prospective buyers and people who you want to visit your site. If you mistakenly market to the wrong audience, then your message will be ineffective. If you know exactly who will be visiting your website, then you can have a site made that fits your audience perfectly. You accomplish this by offering features, functionality, navigation, look-and-feel and messaging that is ideal for your specific audience.

A client of ours wanted to reach the newly retired. The website needed to speak directly to people in their sixties who wanted to learn how to plan their lives now that they had more free time. Since we knew that the audience would be older and may not have the best eyesight any more, we knew in advance that the navigation buttons and copy needed to be in font sizes that were large enough to be read by someone who needed glasses to read. We didn't make the content tiny and therefore frustrating for the site's main audience.

Another example would be if your website's main audience will be 18-25 year-olds. In this case, you'd likely be reaching a market that had sophisticated website usage skills, who were familiar with Web 2.0 and who had very defined expectations. In this case, by knowing all this in advance you would seek a Web firm that specialized in building sites that fit these criteria or that have built similar sites.

A website's audience can be broken down into demographics, psychographics, behaviors, and affiliations.

Dictionary.com defines demographics this way:

The statistical data of a population, esp. those showing average age, income, education, etc.

Psychographics:

The use of demographics to study and measure attitudes, values, lifestyles, and opinions, as for marketing purposes

Behaviors

> **Important: There is no "typical" visitor**
>
> Don't try to come up with the archetype visitor. There is no single type of visitor to any website. There are wide variations among members of any group. For example, although you may determine that women from the ages of 21-35 visit your website the most, understand that these women undoubtedly have very different incomes and backgrounds. When trying to figure out who your website audience is, try to group, but be flexible. You don't want to alienate possible visitors.

People can be identified and grouped by their common behaviors. When determining your audience, look for common behaviors that your site visitors share, both online and in the real world. An example of online behavior that defines a group could be the way people tend to look for information. People who use the Internet every day could be one group, and people who use it only once a week could be another group. Or your website might aim to attract outdoor types who like to hike and camp. In that case, your Web verbiage would greatly differ from those who like big cities and dancing.

Affiliations

People, organizations, or establishments that are associated with one another are known as affiliations. Examples are groups of people who belong to the same church or political group. Affiliations offer another way you can define your website audience.

Know who your market is in advance. This knowledge will help you streamline the website development process, craft more effective messaging and make you more money. Most likely, you already have a good idea who your audience is. If you're an existing business, you can use customer data to help you shape a picture of who buys from you or who is interested in your subject. This is important knowledge to have, not just for the development of your website, but also for your ongoing marketing efforts. If you have records of past customers, it would be well worth it to review them to determine what types of things they have in common. Popular ways to group people are by age, sex, occupation, interests, affiliations, backgrounds, education, income and lifestyles. Try finding commonalities among your existing customers.

If you are creating a new business with a new website, you'll need to do research to determine who your audience is going to be. This is where the Web is very helpful. You can visit competitors' websites and glean from their sites who they think their audience is. You can do searches for market research in your industry as well.

The last two questions you need to answer and record in your Website Plan Document before you begin are about time and money: What's your budget and when do you need it?

Question 3: What is your budget?

Know the upper ceiling that you or your organization is willing to pay. This is the top amount you will pay to have the site completed, functional and live on the Internet.

Pricing in the Web design industry is all over the map, so you're going to have to do your homework on this one. Many different things make up a website, and each feature can be priced differently. Here are the main things you will pay for in a website:

- The graphic design, or the creation of the look-and-feel

- Graphics creation or digital photo manipulation

- Existing clip art or photograph licensing

- The copy writing and proofreading
- The programming of functionality, i.e. forms, e-commerce, forum software, databases, content management software, etc.
- Domain name
- Hosting
- Navigation code
- Information architecture (the organization of the site's information)
- Putting it all together
- Posting it live in the Web

Anyone giving you pricing ought to itemize it so you can compare specific services across vendors.

I also recommend calling or e-mailing a number of Web designers or companies and asking them for ballpark pricing. Some will need a lot more information from you to give you an accurate quote and some may even require that you meet first.

To get around this, insist that you just need a ballpark price range and be prepared to explain to them what your site's purpose is. Remember, you've already answered Question 1, so you ought to have a clear picture of what your site needs to be.

Time frame plus pricing

When you are getting pricing information, also ask for a ballpark time frame they think it will take to complete the project.

Ask business associates or friends how much they paid for their websites. Be sure to obtain a clear picture of what they got for the price. You want to be comparing apples to apples. Finally, you may consider joining a few forums where Web design and development is discussed and ask for typical prices.

Once you have obtained a handful of ballpark price ranges and time frames, you'll have a better idea how realistic your budget is, what you can expect to get for it, and roughly how long it will take.

Your website is like any other major business expense. You usually know in advance what you're going to pay for office rent, what you can afford to pay employees, or how much you plan on spending for equipment. Treat a website in the same way and know how much you can spend in advance. Never leave it open-ended.

Here are the typical ways in which Web designers charge:

- By the project
- By the hour
- By the page and or feature
- Any combination of the above

I think the best deal is finding a vendor who charges by the project (as long as they itemize it) instead of by the hour. If the vendor charges by the hour and hits a snag, ends up taking a long time before you are satisfied with the design, or takes extra time to figure some new technical skill that your site specifically requires, then the hours can add up and cost you a lot.

Question 4: What is your Timeline/Deadline?

The reason you want to have a firm budget and deadline in place before you hire anyone is because this will weed out vendors who can't comply and will help stop you from getting overcharged or strung along. Your goal is to agree in advance what they will charge you and how long it will take, so at the end they don't surprise you with a larger bill or tell you it's going to take another two months to finish.

Determine in advance when you need it done by. Be flexible, but state your absolute deadline in advance and make sure it is in the contract (more on contracts later).

Create a Rough Outline of Your Future Website

After you've answered these four questions, you'll need to create a rough outline of what you want. This ought to be recorded in your Website Plan Document. You're not trying to nail down a specific, detailed and exhaustive description of your future website here. You're simply trying to commit to paper a broad brush-stroke concept of what the site will consist of.

Use the information I provided for you in Chapter 1, "The Fundamentals of a Website," to help you determine what type of site you think will serve your business needs best. In conjunction with this information look at the answers to your first two questions above as well.

This is your chance to be creative. Think of it like you're creating a wish list of the best possible website you would like to have. The sky is the limit. Of course, you may need to eliminate some of the things on this list later based on your budget and timeline. But for now just write down what you think you want to include. Here are four simplified Website Plan Document examples:

Example 1. My New Website

Goal/purpose: Establish a new revenue stream for me by creating a blog and forum website that discusses NASCAR racing. Its main purpose will be to provide information, news and education for all-things-NASCAR. The revenue stream will be realized by selling advertising and AdSense on all pages.

Main Audience: American men between the ages of 15-50. Sub group includes American women in the same age range.

Budget: $3,000

Time frame: 2.5 months

Rough Outline: This site will be a blog that I can update regularly and a forum that anyone can join and discuss whatever they want regarding NASCAR. Besides the home page, blog and forum, I'd like a section that can contain NASCAR articles, a page that describes why I love NASCAR, and a resource center where NASCAR fans can visit to find other NASCAR websites.

Example 2. My New Website

Goal/purpose: Establish a new revenue stream for me by creating an e-commerce website that sells my proprietary gaming software. Its main purpose is to find leads of people who may be interested in buying my software. The revenue stream will be realized by charging people to download and use my software.

Audience: The main audience will be men ages 14-45 who are computer game fanatics from any industrialized nation.

Budget: $1,000

Time frame: 1 month

Rough Outline: The site will have a home page, a Policy and Terms page, an About Us page, a Contact Us page, a section that allows site visitors to demo the software, a software download section where people can buy it or try it for 30 days, a Support section that has a Frequently Asked Questions page and a forum where they can ask me and other users questions regarding the software.

Example 3. My New Website

Goal/purpose: An e-commerce website that sells baby strollers. I'll pocket the profits. Its main purpose is to educate new mothers and in the process sell them baby strollers. The strollers will be drop shipped by various baby stroller vendors that I will set up relationships with once the site is completed.

Audience: The main audience will be American mothers or expectant mothers between the ages of 20-40.

Budget: $8,000

Time frame: 4 months

Rough Outline: The site will have a home page, most likely a Policy and Terms page, an About Us page, a Contact Us page, a library section of original educational materials for mothers, and a storefront with a fully automated e-commerce section that accepts credit cards. I also want to create an online newsletter where I can get people to sign up on my site and allow me to send a monthly newsletter updating them on my offers.

Example 4. Re-vamped Corporate Website

Goal/purpose: We have an old and outdated website for our health care business that needs to be completely re-vamped so we can look more professional, more trustworthy, communicate more easily with our sales force and showcase and sell all our products.

Audience: Hospital purchasing agents, doctors and nurses
Budget: $25,000
Time frame: 6 months
Rough Outline: The site will contain all the content and sections that is on the old site, but all this content will be updated. It will also have two new sections:

1. A password-protected area for our sales force

    a. Sales materials and resources
    b. A CRM (customer relations management) system for logging in every customer contact and interaction

2. An e-commerce storefront that allows site visitors to learn all about each of our products and buy them online if desired

Bear in mind that these four sample Website Plan Documents are simplified. Yours may be more involved and more specific. By creating your Website Plan Document in advance, you are pressing yourself (or your organization) to determine what you want and need at the outset of the project. You are making it much easier to search for an appropriate Web vendor. You are ensuring that each potential Web vendor gives you an accurate quote and that you'll be able to compare proposals. Finally, you're making it crystal clear in advance what you expect the Web vendor to create for you.

The Website Plan Document will keep you, your organization and your Web vendor all on the same page throughout the entire project.

Chapter 4

Begin Your Search

Creating a List of Potential Vendors

Here are the questions you face when you begin your search for a Web vendor:

- Should I hire a local Web vendor or one that is out-of-town?

- If out of town, should they be in my country or could they be located anywhere in the world?

- Should I meet them in person or by phone?

- Should I hire a large firm, a freelancer, or a small business Web vendor?

- Does personality matter?

The answers to these questions will vary with your comfort level and with what the project dictates.

Local or Out-of-Town

The benefits of local vendors are that you can meet the person face to face. This may help you better decide and may weed out people who refuse to meet with you in person or who you don't feel comfortable with. Furthermore, a local person or firm will be able to come to your office to hash out complex aspects of your website project.

For example, if you need a 5-page static website, then there may be no need for the vendor to come to your office. The project is fairly straightforward. However, if you have a 500-

page website that needs to be re-vamped and you are requiring it to be e-commerce enabled and have a catalog of 1000 products, all of which need to be properly entered into the database and website, you may need the vendor to come to your office a few times to work out the details.

The benefit of shopping for out-of-town Web vendors is that the universe you can select from is a lot bigger. This means you can probably find and negotiate a better price and you'll have a larger skill set to choose from. Furthermore, you'll have a better chance of finding a vendor who has completed a project that is similar to your project. But if you go this route, keep in mind that it may take longer to get answers from your phone calls or e-mails and that you'll likely never meet the people working on your pages face to face. Also, time zone differences may make it more challenging to communicate.

My Country or Anywhere

I do not recommend using a Web firm outside the U.S. or Canada if you live in North America. The time zone differences are so large that you can spend up to a day waiting for answers, and oftentimes accents and cultural difference end up making the project harder than it needs to be. Since your look-and-feel and verbiage will directly affect sales and site activity, be sure they are being created by people who totally understand the nuances of your language and audience.

Of course if your audience is going to be mainly from India, then it may be wise to hire an Indian firm. But if your audience is American, then hire an American firm.

In the age of immediate communication, e-mail, scanners and faxes, a thousand miles doesn't mean that much anymore. I don't think it is a big deal if you are based in California and want to hire a vendor in Massachusetts.

Should I meet them in person or by phone?

If all other things are equal, meeting a potential Web vendor in person is best. You can learn so much from actually sitting down with someone and having a face-to-face conversation. If they are associated with a local business, by all means ask them to come to your offices to meet in person. But there are always other factors to consider. For example, if you find a firm that is not local but has experience in your industry and come highly recommended, then that may trump the need to meet them in person first.

Free-lancer, Sole Proprietor or Web Company

A free-lancer or sole proprietor will often charge you less due to their overall lower overhead. There will only be one point of contact, which is important and often very helpful. You'll probably be able to have more personalized service. Of course, if you're considering hiring a one-man band, you'll want to be sure that he or she has skills in design, programming and marketing and is well versed in the Three Pillars of the Web.

A free-lancer is not quite the same as someone who owns a Web vendor business but is the sole employee, often called a sole proprietor. The differences can be subtle, but a person who has an established business as a sole proprietor may be more reliable than a free-lancer. It may be difficult to tell the difference, but if a person uses a name for their business other than their first and last name, if they have a business website and are incorporated and have a tax ID number, then he or she is a sole proprietor.

Important: Check for skill sets

If you are considering hiring one person to do the job, make absolutely sure that the person has skills in all three areas mentioned in Chapter 2, "Digital Graphic Design, Web Programming and Web Marketing." If you hire a Web firm with a larger number of employees, be sure that these three skill sets are well represented in their company.

A Web firm has to pay employees and has more overhead, so expect to pay more for the same project. You may also have to deal with more than one person on a regular basis. They may have a whole roster of clients and not be able to give you the time you require or feel comfortable with. On the other hand, the chances they have skills in all the areas required for a successful website are better. They often have more resources and may have had more clients than a freelance provider. Beware that after you sign the project contract you may be given an account manager whom you haven't met.

Also bear in mind that a Web firm may have you meet with a representative who promises you things that he or she does not fully understand (especially if the person is not technical) and you will later be told they can't fulfill exactly what you need once the programmers discover what's needed. This doesn't happen often but at least be aware of this potential disaster.

This is one of the biggest mistakes people make when hiring a person or company to build them a website. They don't realize in advance that these three skill sets are required to create an effective website presence. Because the Internet is so new and is made up of art, technology and marketing, people who build sites often specialize in only one of these areas.

As I noted in Chapter 2, lots of graphic designers became Web designers before they know much of anything about Web programming or the technical side of the Web. There are also people who are technical experts but don't have a creative bone in their body. And of course there are people who can write excellent Web copy and know a thing or two about marketing but don't know the fundamentals of Web programming or design. Your website builder needs to be well-versed in all of these disciplines or you are not going to get an effective site worth your investment. You'll probably end up getting stuck having to hire another person or firm to fill in the skills needed.

Your job is to ask if they have all these skills and ask for examples of each. If they say they hire sub-contractors for some of these things, ask to see the work of the sub-contractors they plan on hiring for your project. Consider interviewing the sub-contractors as well.

You may be wondering why I am saying that your Web vendor needs marketing skills as well as design and technical skills, even if you plan on hiring another firm for the marketing after the site is built. The reason is that there are many things that can be built into the site that have a direct affect on the marketing.

For example, if you hire a vendor who knows only design and programming and need a Web form built that captures user contact information, they may create a long form with twenty fields for the user to fill out. A vendor with a solid grasp of marketing principles would know in advance that a form with many fields is much less likely to be filled out than a form that has the minimum number of fields.

Another thing a savvy e-marketer will do when building the site is make it search engine friendly from the start. You'd be surprised at how few Web designers know how search engines work and what they look for in a site. A Web vendor who knows e-marketing, including search engine optimization, will usually automatically build your site with search engines in mind.

Ideally you want to hire a free-lancer or sole proprietor who has all these skills or a Web company that has employees who have all these skills.

Does Personality Matter?

In a word, yes. This should be a no-brainer. As you begin to contact each potential Web vendor, make a concerted effort to see if you like how they interact with you. Watch out for ones who act like they know it all, ones who talk with lots of technical jargon that you don't understand, ones who don't ask you many questions, or ones who act superior, laconic or haughty. By examining their personalities while on the phone, in person or even in e-mails, you'll be giving yourself one more data point to help you decide.

Begin Your Search

Now you are armed with lots of useful information on websites and their components, Web designers, Web projects, time lines, budgets, and many other pieces of information that make you an informed buyer. You should also have your Website Plan Document that answers the four main questions and lists the types of things you want to include on your website.

To find a Web vendor (either a freelance Web designer or a company) use these techniques:

- Use Google, MSN Search and Yahoo Search to find a list of Web vendors.

- Ask friends, co-workers, family and business associates for referrals.

- Visit websites you like and your competitors' websites and determine if you can who made their website.

Google, MSN Search and Yahoo Search

If a Web vendor shows up in a search using Google, then at least you know that they have a good grasp of search engine optimization. This of course says nothing about their prices, services, work quality, technical skills, design skills and so forth, but at least they're off to a good start.

Here are a few tips to help you search online more effectively:

1. Never search using one word or two words. Try to use three to seven words. This search rule does follow the law of diminishing returns. Searching using 25 words will probably get you poor results. Look for the "sweet spot" for any given search.

   Example: *website design company in springfield* is better than *web design.*

2. Weed out irrelevant words by using the minus (-) sign next to the word. Since there may be words that appear in your results that are not anything like what you intended, add a minus sign to such words. In the case above, there is a Springfield in numerous states, so you may do this:

Example: *website design company in springfield* -ma if a lot of results are yielding companies in Massachusetts and you're looking for Illinois companies. The "-" deletes "ma" from the results.

3. Use more than one search engine for a wider range of results. Pay special attention to vendors who appear in more than one search engine's results.

4. Consider perusing Web vendor directories that show up in the results. Many websites list Web designers and developers. You can find a wide array of potential vendors and will be able to compare services.

5. Here is a list of keyword phrases you may want to use when searching:

   - *Web design company in Baltimore* (replace "Baltimore" with your city)

   - *Website creation for small business*

   - *Web design and development for high-tech companies* (replace "high-tech" with your industry)

   - *Website building services in Baltimore for high tech companies*

   - *Hire a freelance Web designer specializing in high-tech websites* (replace "high-tech" with your industry)

   - *Hire a Web company in Baltimore for a high-tech website*

   - *Web development directories*

   - *Web marketing and design company lists*

Ask for referrals

Asking friends, co-workers, family and business associates for referrals is always a good strategy when hiring anyone. Be sure to ask if they were satisfied, how they handled requests after the project was completed, whether they thought they got a fair price, and how long the project took.

Visit websites

Are there a couple of websites that you particularly like? Do you enjoy their functionality, ease of use and design? Go to these websites and look in the footer of the home page. The footer is generally the bottom inch or two of the page and often has copyright information and text links pointing to other sections of the site. Often you'll find the company that built the site listed there. Look for "Site Designed By ABC Design," or "An ABC Design Production," or "Site Created by ABC Design." Click on their link or if there is no link, cut and paste the name into Google to find their site.

If you don't see design service's name in the footer, consider calling or e-mailing the company and simply asking who built their site.

You can also look in the footers of your competitor's websites. This may be a good strategy since these Web vendors will already be familiar with your industry, which is always a big plus.

You should have come up with quite a few possible Web vendors to hire using the techniques above. It's all right if the list is rather large; you'll weed them out faster than you can imagine. If you only have a few on your list right now, go back and try to come up with more.

Compile Your List

Now that you have a list, eliminate the ones that don't fit your criteria or your tastes. First, visit each Web vendor's website and check out their design with a critical eye. If you don't like the site's look-and-feel or usability, there's too much of a risk you won't like what they'll do for you either.

Use the following checklist when visiting each potential Web vendor website. Place a check mark in the box next to each question you would answer, "Yes." If a vendor ends up with 6 or more check marks, it has "passed" this test.

Website Checklist for Potential Web Vendors

☐ 1. Do I like the site's overall look-and-feel and design?

☐ 2. Is it easy to navigate through the site, easy to move around in?

☐ 3. Does the navigation make sense?

☐ 4. Is the site free of misspellings, broken links and pages under construction?

☐ 5. Is it easy to find any information I am looking for?

☐ 6. Is there a list of past clients? If so, are any of them in the same industry as mine?

☐ 7. Do I like and connect with the site's writing and content?

☐ 8. Is there a design portfolio? If so, do I mostly like the client website designs?

The last item in the checklist allows you to delve deeper into the potential Web vendor's work. You've rated their website, now it's time to rate the websites they have designed and built.

Apply the following checklist to a number of websites in their portfolio. Try to choose companies that are in the same or similar industries as yours. Place a check mark in the box next to each question you would answer, "Yes." If a vendor ends up with 6 or more check marks, it has "passed" this test.

Website Checklist for Clients of Potential Web Vendors

1 Have they designed, built/coded and marketed these site? ☐yes ☐no

2 Are any of these websites in the same industry as yours? ☐yes ☐no

3 Do I like each site's overall look-and-feel and design? ☐yes ☐no

4 Is it easy to navigate through each site? ☐yes ☐no

5 Does the navigation make sense? ☐yes ☐no

6 Does the navigation setup and functionality vary among sites? ☐yes ☐no

7 Are the sites free of misspellings, broken links and pages under construction? ☐yes ☐no

8 Is it easy to find any information I am looking for? ☐yes ☐no

9 Do I like and connect with the site's writing and content? ☐yes ☐no

Now you ought to have the following:

- Your Website Plan Document—A document that you created that answered the four major questions regarding your new website building project along with a rough outline of the sections and features you want to include in your website.

- A long list of potential Web vendors to choose from and the two checklists associated with each vendor, one for their website and the other for their clients' websites.

- An idea whether you want to go with a one-person freelancer, sole proprietor or a company.

- An idea whether you want to go with a vendor who is out of town or local.

- A general idea of how the personality of the Web vendor will fit with you.

Here's a sample chart to show you how to organize all the information you've accumulated. *(See the Appendix for a blank chart to copy and use.)*

Vendor Name and Website	Local or Out of Town	Person Free-lancer, Sole Proprietor or Company	Did they pass their business website checklist?	Did they pass their clients' websites checklist?	How did you find them?
ABC Web Design www. abcdesign.com	Out of town	Company	Yes	Yes	Google and Yahoo
John Smith www. johnsmith.com	Out of town	Free-lancer	No	Yes	Google
Cool Designs, Inc. www. cooldesign. com	Out of town	Company	No	No	Friend recom- mended
Acme Development www. acmedev.com	Local	Company	Yes	yes	Business associate recom- mended
Ace Web Design www. acewebdesign. com	Local	Sole proprietor	Yes	Yes	Competitor used them

Instructions:

> Enter in all the potential Web vendors you've found so far using all the methods I have described.

> Mark down which ones are local or out of town, and which ones are free-lancers or companies.

> Complete the checklist for each vendor still you your list and then enter "Yes" for each checklist you were able to check at least 75 percent of the questions.

Of course you need a much larger list than this example contains.

Once your list is complete, your next step is to exclude the ones that don't provide what you specifically want. For instance, if you only want to hire locally, then eliminate the first three using the example above. Or if you absolutely loved the clients' website of two vendors, then eliminate the rest. Or if you feel a company suits your needs better than a one-person Web vendor, then you can get rid of all the services except those provided by companies.

Your goal here is to eliminate enough to give you a remaining list of maybe three to six possible Web vendors. Now you contact each one by phone or e-mail and use the information provided in the next chapter to choose the perfect one for you.

Chapter 5

Narrow it Down to One

Steps to Finding the Best Vendor for You

Now it's time to find the Web vendor that is perfect for you and your project. By following these steps, you will be sure to vet each possible Web vendor you're considering and are greatly increasing your chances of getting the best vendor at the best price. Create folders to contain the information of each of these potential Web vendors. Add the proposals into each one as they arrive.

The steps are simple. First, you contact each of the possible vendors on your list. You ask them a series of questions to help you eliminate a few and then send them your website document. They ought to review it to make sure they can effectively help you and that they're appropriate for the project.

While they are reviewing the document, call some of their references. This may help you eliminate a few more.

Next you set up a time to meet with each of them on the phone or in person so that you can convey to them exactly what you want and they can make suggestions to help achieve your website's business goals.

Await each of their formal proposals. After you've received them all, you're ready to make your decision based on a lot of useful and relevant information for each one. You ought to be able to get it down to just two vendors at this point.

Contact these finalists again and explain to them that you've narrowed it down and total project price will determine the project winner. Ask them if they can bid again with a lower price. Then make your final decision.

Pricing

Understanding and obtaining fair pricing can be a major challenge. Notice that I didn't suggest finding pricing information for each potential Web vendor's website while compiling your initial list. This is because many vendors don't publish pricing on their websites, and for good reason. Most projects are customized, and unless the vendor understands exactly what you want and need, publishing pricing on a website they have built is a waste of time for them and you.

Let me explain this further, using the house analogy again. If you visited a home-building company's website, it would be futile to list how much they charge for building a house. Ranch, cape or colonial? Carpets or hardwood floors? Porches, balconies, garage? How many windows? What kind of kitchen? How many bedrooms and bathrooms? How many square feet? I could go on and on.

There are so many variables, options, sub-options, and configurations of options, that it's best if the company first learns what you want, then gives you a price. The same goes for building a website. Don't expect an accurate price quote until you've had a chance to explain in detail what you want and need.

Since there are also many variables, features, options and configurations for websites, there are many ways that building one can be priced. Some Web companies get very creative in the way they price things. So be careful.

You'll also need to pay attention to how you are comparing prices across Web vendors. If all the vendors you're considering charge by the hour, then you'll be comparing apples to apples. But if one vendor charges by the features and another charges by the page, you don't have a good comparison.

A long time ago, I worked for a Web design firm that charged $100 for each page it created for a client. So if you wanted a home page, product page, company description page and a contact page, you would pay $400 total for the site to be built for you. If you wanted an e-commerce site, had 2,000 products and wanted a separate page for each product, you'd be billed $20,000 for a website using this pricing model.

Other Web vendors will charge per feature. A basic site that includes four pages might have a set fee of $500 for example, a contact form would cost $300, a storefront with ten products would cost $2,000, and a blog would cost $1,000, and so on.

Suppose you understand the pricing per feature, but the next vendor you're considering charges by the hour. How can you compare pricing then?

The answer is to explain to each prospective vendor that you're considering several possible vendors that are using different pricing models. Ask them to resubmit a price to you that matches the other models. Ask them to give you a total project price based on hours spent. Or ask them to give you a price based on features—or whichever system works best for you.

Keep in mind that you want to hire a firm or free-lancer that's flexible, so if they refuse to give you another pricing method, then maybe that's indicative of the hardball way they work.

Another thing to look for in pricing is payment terms. Each proposal you end up receiving ought to have payment terms clearly marked. Beware of a vendor that asks you to pay everything up front. It is typical to pay half of the total price up front and the rest upon final website delivery. That way, you're both taking an equal risk. If they split it up into three or four payments, that is fine, too.

Finally, be sure you understand exactly what each feature costs. In other words, know how much it costs to create a home page, how much they charge for programming a contact form, or how much they charge for integrating a forum or blog into the site. If they charge by the hour, then determine how long each item will take to complete.

Here are the steps to take once you have developed a list of vendors you feel could handle the site creation job for you and your business:

Step 1: Make First Contact with Web Vendors on Your List

From the moment you make first contact with each vendor you need to pay attention to the interaction, how they communicate with you and how they act overall. You should have a list of three to six possible Web vendors now and your goal is to narrow the field to one, two, or three. The information you get in your first phone call or e-mail can sometimes be enough to eliminate a few.

For instance, if you e-mail the firm and they don't get back to you for three days, maybe they are too busy to give you good service. Or if you call one and they say they charge a flat rate for any website and that they use ready-made website templates before you've even had a chance to tell them what you're specifically looking for, then maybe you need to cross them off your list, too.

A file for each potential vendor

Create a separate file for each possible vendor for notes, their answers to your questions and the e-mails they send you.

However, if you call them and speak to a person who is polite, professional, helpful and pleasant, asks you a lot of relevant questions and seems genuinely interested in your project, then they ought to stay on your list.

Here are the topics you want to cover in your first interaction with each Web vendor:

- Ask what their usual protocol is for creating a proposal and taking on new clients.

- Ask if you can get a couple of client references. If they say "no" to this request, cross them off your list.

- Ask them if they have the time available now to take you on as a client. If they say "no" to this request, cross them off your list.

- Ask each one that you like if you can fax or e-mail your Website Plan Document. Ask them to get back to you with a proposal that contains a price range and time frame for project completion. If they say "no" to this request, cross them off your list.

- Ask them if they can meet you in person (if they're local) or on another phone call to go over your Website Plan Document you plan on sending them after they've had a chance to review it. If they say "no" to this request, cross them off your list.

Step 2: Distribute your Website Plan Documen

Be sure each Web vendor on your list receives your Website Plan Document. This will be a bit help in making the proposals uniform and helping you evaluate them.

Step 3: Contact each Web vendor's client references

After you've made contact with all of your possible Web vendors and they've each sent you a few previous client references, call or e-mail the previous clients. Here is a list of questions you ought to ask them:

- Did they meet your deadlines?

- Were they flexible with you?

- Were they responsive to your suggestions and questions?

- Did they fix your problems promptly?

- Did they work within the original budget or surprise you with higher fees mid-project or at the end of the project?

- Did they set and meet realistic goals for your project?

- Would you hire this firm again for another business website?

Put the answers you obtain into each of your potential Web vendor's file.

Here is another opportunity to help you think about eliminating one or more from your list. If one of the references isn't great, consider crossing the vendor off your list.

Step 4: After they've had a chance to review your document, set up a time and meet each Web vendor in person or on the phone.

Advance details result in a better proposal

The proper way for a potential Web vendor to initiate a new website creation project is to meet with you in person or on the phone to discuss all the details once they know what you want. They do this to help them better prepare an accurate, written proposal.

Whether you meet with them in person or on the phone, this will be another chance for you to evaluate how they interact with you. Pay attention to how they receive your ideas, how knowledgeable they seem, how easy it is to ask them questions and talk to them—or whether they come off pompous and arrogant or trying to dazzle you with technical jargon. Also be sure that they don't suggest a lot of bells and whistles on your website for the sake of charging you more or so they can indulge in their technical and design skills for no apparent benefit to you.

That last point is important, because sometimes you'll be considering a Web vendor who is really good at graphic design. They may want to over-design your site, or they may talk mostly about the design at the expense of the site's intended functionality. People like this may indulge in their "art" and pay less attention to your needs.

Or you may be considering a person or firm that specializes in programming and wants to offer you all kinds of creative functionality that would cost you a lot. They may like to indulge in their technical skills at the expense of design or marketing. Pay attention. You're looking for a vendor who offers a balance of all three pillars of the Web: design, technical and marketing.

Here are topics you ought to cover when you meet with the prospective vendor in person or on the phone:

- Can they handle all three parts of website development: design, technical, and marketing? They ought to have digital design skills and experience, technical skills other than only knowing HTML, and Web marketing skills and experience.

- Do they know how to market the site when it's done? (See Chapter 9—"After it's Built, You HAVE to Market It" to learn more about the kinds of marketing they should know)

- If yes, what can they do, and is this included in the project cost?

- Are they flexible and responsive to your project input?

- Do they communicate with you in a professional manner, not talking down to you or trying to impress you with their superior skills?

- What types of problems could change the scope of the project and therefore the price?

- How do they handle mid-stream changes?

- If there is a mid-project change that you initiate, how will they charge you? If they attempt to make a mid-project change that they suggest, will you have to pay?

- Where do they get their images? Do they photograph images themselves that they plan on including on your site? Or do they use royalty-free stock photography?

- How do they handle making site edits and updates later on after the project is finished? Unless you hire a webmaster or a person with Web technical skills you'll need a way to make updates to your site after the project is finished.

- If you need things changed or website updates done, will they do this for you? If so, is this included in the project cost, or how will they charge you?

- Are they going to build you a system where non-technical people can update the website in the future? Or will they integrate a third-party software system that allows you to do this? Is this included in the project cost?

Producing revenue, a high priority

Since this is a going to be a website for your business and your business needs to make money, make sure that the Web vendors you're considering talk about how the site will be constructed in order to optimally produce revenue. For example, if the potential vendor only talks about designing it and never mentions revenue-producing aspects of the site, then cross that provider off your list.

Since you've prepared only a rough outline of your future website, use this meeting as an opportunity to hear what each vendor suggests for the project. They may have some good ideas. They may suggest functionality or website features you never thought of that will help your site achieve your business goals.

Also keep in mind that this may be the last time you have a long conversation with them before you make your decision, so be sure to ask them all the questions you can think of, take notes, and be ready to find reasons to eliminate one or more.

After you've met with the prospective vendors, each of them should have a clear picture of what you want. Now you await their proposals.

Pay more attention to the ones who create and send back to you a formal proposal. Vendor 1 may simply reply in an e-mail with a price and end date only. Vendor 2 may create and mail you a document that not only provides an itemized price range and time frame, but also a detailed outline for how they are going to complete your new website. Obviously Vendor 2 is more attractive than Vendor 1 in this case.

Once you've met with each vendor in person or on the phone, spoken to a few of their past clients, and received their proposals, you ought to have enough information to determine the one you want to hire for your project. If there is still more than one possible Web vendor at this point, you may want to call the ones you're considering and ask for more details about what they plan on doing to help you in your project.

Step 5: Negotiate a Better Price

This step is optional. If you have found the perfect match and they've asked for a price that's in your budget, you're ready to hire them. But just in case, it's still a good idea to attempt to negotiate the price down. If they don't budge, at least you've tried.

If you still have two or more on your list and you can't decide which one to choose, consider having them compete with each other on price and whoever gives the better final price gets the job. Contact each of the finalists again and explain to them that you've narrowed it down to a few and the total project price will determine the project winner. Ask them if they can bid again with a lower price.

Price List

Each proposal ought to have an itemized price list. If the vendor doesn't include one, ask them to itemize all the things they plan on doing to finish your project and have them send you a revised proposal.

Another way to negotiate a better price is by going over each item in their proposal and asking them and yourself if you really need each feature. There may be one or more features, types of functionality, or specific pages that you don't necessarily need, and if you eliminate them, you may be able to land within your budget. To help you determine which features you may not need, go back to your Website Plan Document and review what you stated as your site's main purpose. If a feature doesn't help this purpose or is questionable, consider getting rid of it.

Most functionality features have already been created using third-party software and can be purchased and integrated into a new site easily and inexpensively. Examples of functionality features are shopping carts, blogs, forums, forms, surveys, and content management systems—basically anything that requires programming other than HTML. If a Web vendor says they can program (or code) a feature for you, insist that they explore integrating an existing package that does the same thing.

A shopping cart is the software that displays products, pricing and description, stores a user's choices till checkout and then accepts contact and credit card information. Hundreds of shopping carts are in existence today, and it is highly unlikely that you need one specifically programmed for you. If a vendor suggests that route, consider it a red flag.

Consider third-party software

Don't let a Web vendor reinvent the wheel by programming a feature that is readily available elsewhere. This will cost you money you don't need to spend. Ask to use third-party software for any functionality you require.

Of course if you have a billion dollar company that has a highly specialized market and set of products, then you may require a completely customized shopping cart. Keep in mind that programming features from scratch usually costs the most. In addition, they're time-consuming and require specialized skills. Web vendors may want to create a "custom" functionality feature especially for you so they can make more money on the project. You need to realize that most of these things have already been created and can be inserted or integrated into a website fairly easily and less expensively than programming it all over again.

Based on the above, a good way to negotiate a better price is to look at all the functionality features of the site that require programming and ask the vendor to find an existing third-party product that you can license and they can integrate to save money. If you know that these third-party software packages exist, and you let them know that you're aware of their existence, you may be able to talk them down in price.

Here's a final checklist for ensuring you're choosing the right Web vendor from your list:

Final Web Vendor Checklist

☐ Does the Web vendor have design, technical and marketing skills?

☐ Did they send a formal written proposal?

☐ Do I like their overall personality?

☐ Does it seem like they'll want to add unnecessary bells and whistles?

☐ Did they tell me where they get their images?

☐ Are they easy to get in touch with?

☐ Did they answer my e-mails and voice-mails in a timely manner?

☐ Does the proposal contain an itemized price list?

☐ Did I get the best possible price from them?

☐ Did I get a firm end date?

Close the Deal

After you've narrowed your list of prospective website vendors down to one, you're ready to close the deal. You ought to receive a contract from the Web vendor that explains exactly what they are going to do for you, how they handle payment, how they handle project changes, and includes the itemized final price and completion date. Often this contract is part of the formal proposal they sent you.

Read the fine print. Be sure to pay special attention to how they handle mid-project changes. Have an attorney review the contract and be sure you keep a copy of the contract that you *both* have signed.

Chapter 6

What You Need to Provide

Bringing Content to your Website

To help the project go more smoothly, avoid delays and get it completed more quickly, you can take several steps after you sign the contract. Although the Web vendor you've chosen has gone through your thorough selection process because you've used all the advice in this book, they are not mind readers.

They need you to provide them with content, a navigation outline, a style guide, images, a logo, media files and anything else you want to include on your site. Even if you have nothing, work closely with them as you develop most of these items. Otherwise, you'll be handed a website at the end that is nothing like you initially envisioned. Or you'll waste valuable time going back and forth till they hit upon what you had originally wanted. Chapter 8 will explain how to create these items for your Web vendor to use.

Content

You know your business the best, and you ought to be an expert in your business. You know what you want to include on your site. You know what you want to communicate to your website visitors. And you most likely have a great idea who your market is and how to talk to them. So you'll need to help provide the written content.

You may have hired a Web vendor who offers Web copy-writing services as part of your contract. You'll still need to provide rough drafts of the messages you want to include on your website. Your vendor will massage your content, make it readable online, and integrate it into the site in the best way for online consumption. But be ready to provide them content.

People have no patience online. They have itchy trigger fingers and click away to another site after only a couple of seconds. There are studies that show people lasting only three seconds on a home page, and if they don't see what they want, they click their "back" button and they're gone!

This means that Web copy needs to be succinct. Avoid large blocks of copy, or it will never be read. Use bold words, headlines, subheadlines, bullets and indentations to break text up. Your main website pages' copy ought to be short and sweet.

Your deeper pages, ones that are more than one or two clicks away from the home page for instance, can be more involved. If a website visitor likes your initial

Quality content is essential

Written collateral materials ARE NOT the same as website content. Many organizations make the mistake of lazily grabbing old brochures, catalogs, magazine advertisements or pamphlets and throwing them up on their website. Don't make this mistake. Allow your Web vendor to rework the copy so it's appropriate for the Internet. Or hire a Web copywriter to create the content or modify your old collateral materials so that the text fits on the Web.

content and then chooses to dig deeper and is looking for very specific and unique content, that's when you can include larger amounts of text.

See Chapter 7—"What Makes a Website Great: Rules to Follow and Qualities to Include" for more information on proper Web copy writing.

A Navigation Outline

Not only do you need to provide written content for your Web vendor, you'll also need to decide what major sections your site will have. You can make these decisions yourself, with your marketing team, or with your Web vendor. But you should make them as soon as possible, before serious work on your website begins.

Think of this process as the buttons on your navigation bar. For example, you may want to break your site into the company description section, the resources section and the products section. In this scheme, you may have a navigation bar with three buttons: Company, Resources and Products. Under each of these sections can be sub-categories. So it may look like this:

Company

> About Us
> Contact Us
> Management

Resources

> White Papers
> FAQs
> Support
> Forum

Products

> Downloads
> Books

By determining these sections at the onset of the project, you are in essence creating a website outline. You can then use this outline to help you gather and create content for each section and subcategory.

See Chapter 8—"The Planning and Implementation of a Successful Business Website."

A Style Guide

An important item on your list to send the Web vendor is a style guide. This is a document that lists the requirements for how your site will appear, a guide to what makes up the site's look-and-feel. If you don't provide this, then you're taking the chance that the Web vendor will incorrectly make it up for you.

They may be way off the first or second time around, causing them to have to go back and try again. This causes project completion delays and sometimes higher costs. The more you define for them in advance, the less guessing they'll need to do. A style guide ought to contain the following:

- Your primary color of choice and one or two secondary, complementary colors

  If possible, supply the RGB (Red, Green, Blue) numbers or their hexadecimal equivalents. This way, they are producing the exact color you suggest and there is no need for interpretation. Pick from a list of Web-safe colors. That way you'll be assured that your website visitors' computers will be able to render the color you intend. (Do a search online for "Web safe colors" to find a list). Refer to Chapter 8 to help you choose your website colors.

- Your font sizes and styles

  Be careful on this one. First, never use more than two main fonts on your site. Also, don't use obscure fonts. Unless you choose a common computer font, you can't be sure that the computers of your website visitors have the same font to render. In other words, they may see different fonts than the ones you intended. If you're not sure of fonts, ask your Web vendor to make some suggestions, but let them know you want them to look the same on all computers.

- A list of websites you like

  This should be a short list, and rank them if you can. They ought to be websites that look and feel good to you. Also, they don't need to be your competitors' sites, they can be in the same industry or completely unrelated.

- Any other specifics on what you want your site to look like

This may include how text is broken up from images, how long you want each page, if different sections will have slightly different but related looks, and anything else you can think of.

Important: Ask for cross-platform tests

Make sure you ask your Web vendor to test the way your site looks across all browsers and platforms.

Cross-browser and platform compatibility are important to consider when creating your style guide. In other words, be sure your site looks the same in the two most popular browsers today, Internet Explorer and Firefox. Also be sure that it looks the same whether using a PC or a Mac. By using Web-safe colors and standard fonts, you're helping to ensure this.

You should use a CSS (cascading style sheet). This is a Web document that has the extension .css and defines things like colors, font sizes and weights, how links appear, background colors, table sizes and anything else to do with a website's appearance. This file can than be referenced by each page in your website.

The two main benefits for using a CSS file are as follows:

1. You make each page's HTML code cleaner and less dense. If you define your styles on each page, you end up with large blocks of style code (embedded in the HTML source code) in the beginning of your page. This makes it harder to edit and makes it take longer to load in a user's browser. A CSS file allows you to take the style code out of every page's source code and store the information in a separate file.

2. You have the ability to change the entire site's style by changing only one file. Let's say you wanted to change the font your site uses. If you use a CSS style sheet, you just change the font definition once, and the new look propagates throughout your entire site. Otherwise you have to make changes on every page of your site. Of

course you don't need to create the CSS file; simply ask your Web vendor to create and include one in your site.

Images

Images are an important part of your website. They convey things that words can't do. Keep in mind that images ought to invoke business-appropriate emotions in your visitors. You may not have any images to supply the Web vendor. In this case, try to be as specific as possible in explaining what kinds of images you want them to include.

Or you may have images to include from your collateral and advertising materials. All images must be in digital format before they can be used on a website, so you or the vendor may need to scan images if you just have them on paper.

You will also need to provide a digital version of your logo. Supply them with the largest logo you can with the highest resolution. This way, when they shrink it down to fit your website, it will maintain its clarity and detail. If you need them to design a new logo for you, expect to pay more.

All image files that are on a website need to be one of two main file extension types: .jpg or .gif. (There are others, but these two are the main ones.)

Media Files

Media files include audio and video files, and anything else other than text and static images.

Possible Third-Party Software Products

This is an optional category. You may want to conduct your own search for possible third-party software that you can have the Web vendor integrate into your site. Use the same search engine searching techniques explained in Chapter 4 to find vendors who provide out-of-the-box or turnkey solutions that can be integrated into any website. Then provide a list of these vendors to your Web vendor.

Now, before the project gets started, take time to think through what you really want. There may be other special things such as interactive calendars, price calculators, or registration forms that you want to include on your website. Again, to use the house-building analogy, if you decide you want four bedrooms instead of three halfway through the project, adding that fourth bedroom is going to cost much more time and money than it would have if you had planned it that way from the start.

The more you define your project in advance, the less guesswork the Web vendor has to do, the less time and money will be spent, and the closer the finished project will be to what you originally wanted.

Now that you've found the best Web vendor for creating your new website and you clearly know what you'll need to provide them with, you're ready to begin the planning and implementation phase of your project. You'll work closely with the vendor you hired in this phase.

Before you start the process you'll need an excellent grasp of what constitutes a great website and what makes a business website successful. Buckle your seat belt and get ready to read Chapter 7, an in-depth chapter that explains all the keys to a great website. Then we'll look at the best way to plan the site and work with your Web vendor to manifest the best business website possible.

SECTION 3

THE PLANNING AND IMPLEMENTATION OF A SUCCESSFUL BUSINESS WEBSITE

Now that you know what websites are made of and have hired the perfect Web vendor to help you with your project, you're ready to create a detailed plan for its development. Once you have the blueprint in hand, you'll be able to implement the actual creation of your new site. Expect to work closely with your Web vendor during this entire process. By following the suggestions in this section, you will greatly increase your chances of ending up with a successful business website that meets your goals.

In a sense, the definition of a great website is rather simple. Remember the four questions I recommended that you answer before you begin your website building project? The very first question was, *"What will be the site's goals and purpose?"* If your website effectively achieves your goals and purpose, consider your website great. A successful business website increases your bottom line, augments your business, and achieves your business goals.

If someone asked you what Internet company you consider as the most successful in the world, which one comes to mind? Most would say Google, and they'd be correct. That company made it through the Internet bubble explosion, and now are valued in the billions of dollars. They have done many things right and have set the standard for the Web in many areas.

(If the story of Google even mildly interests you and you want to learn the extent of their reach and how they got there, I recommend reading the book, *The Search: How Google and Its Rivals Rewrote the Rules of Business and Transformed Our Culture*.)

Have you ever considered the design of Google's website? It is one of the simplest and cleanest home pages in existence. We can all learn from this. You and your Web vendor ought to be chanting this mantra through the entire planning and building phase of your new website: Clean Simple Easy, Clean Simple Easy, Clean Simple Easy. Say it over and over again. Sing it on the way to office; chant it at the meeting with your

Web people. Heck, I'd even make a sign and hang it up over your computer.

People hate complicated websites that make them think too much. They hate feeling confused. They hate feeling stupid. They hate wasting their time. Many competing websites are a literal click away. People have itchy back button fingers.

Google is an excellent example of a great website because it is clean looking, simple to learn and easy to use. Their home page has nothing on it except for the search box, a handful of links giving other search options, a couple more links to other parts of the site, and their logo. That's it. The links are text, blue and underlined. Ninety percent of the home page is white space. It's about as clean as possible. And although they have been tempted to add all kinds of things to the home page, from advertising to news, they have refrained all these years, and for good reason: cleanliness online is paramount. The home page is so clean that it loads in less than a second. And the search results you get come back to you in lightening speed, wasting none of your time.

The site is simple to learn how to use as well. It uses Web conventions that include a search box and button. Enter in the word or words you're searching for and click the "Google

Search" button. The only other option is the "I'm Feeling Lucky" button, that's it.

There is no guessing when you arrive at Google's site. Search for something or click on one of the few links. There are no ambiguous buttons, no strange navigation, and you don't need to do any extra thinking to accomplish your goal of finding something on the Web.

One of the reasons Google has been so successful is because of its clean, simple and easy website. Although there is a lot of code and complicated databases and architecture behind the scenes, Google's functionality is presented to the user in the easiest, most usable way possible, giving immediate feedback for every action a user takes.

If you're committed to building a great website that will improve your business, make every effort to plan and manage the creation of a clean, simple and easy-to-use website. Your Web vendor or your IT people may want to create a site that has complicated technical interfaces or wacky and creative designs that follow no conventions. They may want to do this because it's more fun for them to create or because it takes longer so they can charge you more. Don't give in! Hold your ground. You're not building a website to please the vendor or your technical people; you're building it to make money.

Start with the end in mind. A website needs to increase your business's bottom line. It needs to generate leads and sales for you. Whatever your specific website goals may be, the end result you want is to make more money. Every decision about your future website needs to be made with this in the forefront.

Chapter 7

What Makes a Website Great

Rules to Follow and Qualities to Include

While writing this book, I received an e-mail that advertised a compilation of radio, TV and magazine contacts for promoting non-fiction books. "Perfect," I thought. "I'm writing a non-fiction book right now and would love to get my hands on a list of people I could contact to help me promote my book to a wide audience!"

One strike, however, because it was an unsolicited e-mail that I never signed up to receive. (See Chapter 9 to learn more about avoiding sending out spam). I figured I should check the site out anyway since it was something I really could use.

When I got to the site it looked like Ralphy the senior from the local high school had designed and built it between make-out sessions with Susie in the school library. It was awful looking. It had ugly shades of brown, the text was way too close to the margins, there were spelling mistakes everywhere, five different fonts and font colors were used, and many of the images were broken. Strike two and three.

I just didn't trust the site. It felt like a scam. There was an e-mail address for a contact but no street address or phone number. And when I clicked on the "Order Now" link, it brought me to a page that asked for all my personal contact information with no explanation of what I needed to do next.

Did I get to download the list as a .pdf? Or would they send me a copy in the mail? Did they take my credit card on the next screen or did I have to send a check? The site was confusing, and I had to think too much. I didn't trust the site and had no way of contacting them. The order process did not follow

Web conventions and didn't explain how the process worked. The site looked shoddy and sloppy. They lost a sale because the site broke so many rules, and I'm sure they've lost many sales because of this.

Don't let that be the fate of your business website. Follow time-proven, specific rules and make sure that your site has these exact qualities.

Great Website Rules

Your goal is to create a website that visitors will readily find and that will benefit them in some way. A great website needs to...

- Establish trust;

- Make the visitor's life better in some way;

- Clearly show your visitors the way to accomplish their goals without being confusing.

- Offer the visitor a clean, simple and easy experience.

- Help visitors easily find what they need and then ask them to take an action.

- Offer a clean, simple and easy experience.

- Avoid making the user think unnecessarily.

- Follow established Web conventions.

- Make you and your business look professional.

- Pass the AIDA test: Attention, Interest, Desire, Action.

If you expect to accomplish your website goals and make money with your website, follow these rules with every page on your site.

Let's take a closer look at each of these important rules, why they need to be followed, and how to do it.

Establish trust

One of the biggest roadblocks users need to hurdle is the trust factor. The Web can be a cold, nameless, faceless landscape. The newness of the Web also contributes to a low level of trust. Typing in your credit card number and sending it off into cyberspace without ever speaking to someone requires a leap of faith.

If a website seems untrustworthy, people are not likely to buy from you online. They will also be less likely to offer you contact information if you ask for it.

One way to establish trust is to be sure there are no spelling or grammar mistakes and no broken links. If you're careless with your site, the visitor may conclude that you would be careless with your products, services, customer service, returns and anything else that you do.

Another way to build trust is by joining trusted programs that allow you to display their banner or seal on your website. There is one called Trust Guard. Other examples include BBBOnline (the Better Business Bureau), VeriSign, Thawte, Square Trade, Scan Alert and many more.

Clear guarantees also build trust. Visitors will be reassured if they understand that they can return what they buy from your website for a full refund if they don't like it. Don't underestimate how important trust is to people online.

Make the visitor's life better

If your site helps your visitors achieve their goals, find what they want, learn something new, and add to their world without frustrating them, then you're headed in the right direction. Ask yourself if your site adds to each visitor's life or takes away from it. If you frustrate users, insult them, or waste their time, you're missing the mark. We'll investigate this more in the next couple of rules.

Clearly show visitors the way to accomplish their goals

Web users are goal orientated. They visit a site to get something done. They may need information in researching a product, service or company. They could be ready to buy something. Or they may be studying different perspectives and opinions.

Understand in advance what your website visitors need to accomplish at your site. Once you understand this, it's your job to ensure they can do it easily, simply, quickly, without having to think. Don't make your site confusing. Approach the draft of your new site with an objective mind, specify your goal, and attempt to accomplish it. Note how easy or hard it is to do. Ask a couple other people who are not in your company or industry to do the same and note how hard it is for them.

Help visitors find what they need; ask for action

Since Web users are goal orientated, it's vital to give them clear and simple ways in which they can take the various actions they want to take. Unless you ask visitors to take an action, you're wasting your efforts. Even if you simply offer information and don't sell anything online, you're leaving dollars on the table if you don't ask them for their contact information to market to them later.

But in order for them to get to the point of taking an action, they need to find it first. Make the path easy for them.

Website users can be broken down into two types of searching groups, the search box users, and the link followers.

Search box users enter the key words in a box to find exactly what they're looking for. Your website may benefit from having its own search engine. Google offers a free one as part of their AdSense program. There are many other online services that offer search functions that you can integrate into your website, often without any need for technical knowledge. You can develop one in-house as well.

Link followers click on a button or a highlighted set of words that take them to their destination. Each linking device should be self-evident and easy to use for viewers searching for information on your site. More on this later.

Think of your website as a retail store. When customers enter the front door of the store they need to find what they are looking for easily and quickly. They follow signs hanging over the aisles or ask an employee to lead them to their goal. The store owners have organized their space to funnel people through the store in a way that maximizes sales. They place the best-selling items up front, they make the items on sale obvious, and they put the impulse items near the checkout, just to name a few examples of how stores are set up to make it easy to buy from them.

Your site needs to do the same. Make the signs to the various sections clear and easy to follow. Make the site's search function easy to use. Provide feedback for the actions they take. Don't lead them down dead ends with no way to get back.

People in a store can generally sense where they are at all times in the store. Knowing where the front door is, for example, gives them a sense of direction while wandering the store. A website is different because there is no built-in sense of direction or location. It's your job to provide one.

Making the site's navigation consistent on every page is a great way to ease the search for information from page to page. Try offering bread crumbs, small links that list how a person goes to any page. For instance, an inner page of a website may be three steps away from the home page and contain three small links towards the top of the page that read, Home > Products > Buy Now. Those are bread crumbs.

Page titles also help with providing a sense of location. Be sure to center your title over the page's entire content or at least make it large enough and towards the top enough to clearly identify to the user where they are.

Another good practice is to highlight the link or button in the navigation that represents the page they are currently on. So if your site has a navigation bar that contains a Home link, an About Us link and a Contact Us link, and the visitor is on the About Us page, make that link in the navigation bar stand out from the other two to tell the visitor they are there.

A good book to read about the subject of retail stores and customer behavior is Paco Underhill's *Why We Buy.*

Offer a clean, simple and easy experience

When building each page, always ask yourself if you're providing the cleanest, simplest and easiest way for visitors to accomplish their goals. Needless to say, their goals and your goals ought to line up.

They want to find and buy a widget that fits their needs, and you want them to buy that widget and tell their friends. If they perceive the entire experience in a good light, they are more likely to see it through to the end and buy from you, more likely to come back to buy more, and more likely to tell their friends.

Don't make the user unnecessarily think

One of my favorite Web design and usability bibles is called *Don't Make Me Think*, by Steve Krug. The title says it all. This is such a simple concept, but way too many websites miss it completely. Steve Krug likens website visitors to motorists driving sixty miles per hour on the highway. Cyclists don't stop to examine each billboard. Your website is like those billboards. People don't read every word on your site, nor do they read directions because they don't feel they have the time. An easier and simpler website is just a click away. If you make someone have to think to use your site, they'll leave. Krug says to make things self-evident or at least self-explanatory.

Follow established Web conventions

It's a long-standing Web convention to make clickable words blue and underlined. I am amazed at sites that include links that are the same color as the rest of the text and are not underlined. It's like an Easter egg hunt to find a working link on these sites. Don't do this. Don't try to be cute. Don't let your Web designer talk you into being different because "it looks cool." You're trying to make money by making your website visitors' lives easy, not by being "cool."

If I start to feel like I don't know how to use a site, or I start to get confused at the functionality, I simply click the back button and try another site. After all, there's no shortage of other websites out there that can most likely meet my needs.

People scan or just glance at your website pages. They stay on a page for mere seconds and if the way in which they want to accomplish their goals is not painfully obvious, they leave.

Make you and your business look professional

Building a website that appears to represent a professional organization is an obvious way to built trust and attract visitors. Obvious or not, many websites miss the mark and pay the consequences. A website can be designed and presented in such a way that a sole proprietor will seem equal to companies with hundreds of employees. Be sure the site is clean and its architecture is well thought out. See Chapter 7 for more on this.

Be sure you don't have spelling or grammar mistakes, and weed out all broken links. Make every page's navigation, colors and look-and-feel consistent. Use the best graphics you can. Visit sites in your industry or a related industry and visit competitors' sites. Use them as benchmarks for what constitutes *professional* in your space.

Pass the AIDA test

As I've mentioned many times already, the online world is no different from the "real" world when it comes to human behavior and buying. A successful sale depends on attracting the **Attention** of prospective buyers, it needs to stimulate their **Interest,** then their **Desire** to buy. Then it needs to invite them to take an **Action** such as making the purchase.

The world of sales knew this long before the emergence of the Web. The online sales process needs to pass the AIDA test as well. Every page of your site needs to attract the attention of the visitor long enough to stimulate interest. Then the page needs to create a strong desire in the visitor to take action. For the visitor to take the action it needs to be clearly defined and easy to do. Finally, the action taken needs to result in satisfaction by providing the visitor with a result that is exactly what was expected.

When your Web vendor presents you with a draft of the home page, an inner page, or a site section, use the "Great Website Rules" list to determine if the rules are being followed effectively. If they aren't, figure out why not and make adjustments before you finalize anything. Far better to be doing this while your Website is being created than when it's already live and being viewed around the globe.

For example, if you have an e-commerce storefront or a page that offers a free demo of your product in exchange for the visitor's contact information, ask yourself, "Is it self-evident and easy for my visitors to find these pages? Do I establish trust on my site that allows visitors to feel comfortable buying from me or giving me their contact information? Does the home page clearly point people to these pages? Does the site make it easy for visitors, regardless of which page they used to enter, find these pages? Do these pages clearly ask visitors to take an action? Do these pages pass the AIDA test?"

Great Website Qualities

Let's now consider the qualities that make up a great website. Your website will be a winner if you make sure it excels in each of the following areas.

Design and Content

- Use Web conventions

- Appealing to the eye

- An appropriate look-and-feel

- Consistency

- Clear navigation labels

- A search function

- Quality, original content

- Well-written copy

- User-oriented content and functionality

- Text, not just images or buttons

- Content information

Use Web Conventions

If you create a website that is unique in every respect so that no one knows how to use it, all you'll accomplish is frustrating your users and driving them away.

The Web has borrowed most of its conventions from print media. These conventions include large headlines, smaller sub-headlines and even smaller text. The logo is in the top left-hand corner or centered on most sites. The logo is usually clickable and brings you back to the site's home page. Links are blue and underlined.

Don't try to be different for the sake of being different. There are many ways to present a creative website, but the basics ought to follow Web conventions. If your site exists to help the user and make you money, then your best bet is to follow Web conventions.

Appealing to the eye

Appeal is obviously a subjective matter. Something may be appealing to one person and horrid to the next. Chapter 7 explained how to determine who your audience is. Refer back to question 2 in your Website Plan Document and try to match the look-and-feel of your site with what you think would be appealing to them, not necessarily to you.

An appropriate look-and-feel

Your site's look-and-feel should be appropriate to your business and audience. If you're an accounting firm, your site may serve you best by having an air of trust and seriousness to. If your site is a children's birthday party site, color, and a feeling of fun and excitement would probably work best.

Consistency

When the look-and-feel completely changes from one page to another in a website, I think I am visiting another site, another company, a partner or subsidiary. I get confused. The lack of consistency screams poor planning and often results from tacking on new sections after the original site was built. This can lead to design-drift with visitors scratching their heads with one hand and clicking to get away with the other.

If you decided to run a traditional ad campaign that used three different creative ads, would each one look totally different? The answer is "No." Using the same fonts, the same colors and keeping the general look-and-feel consistent are fundamental to presenting a unified, dependable, and congruent image to your visitors. If your look-and-feel is all over the place, your potential customers may think your company or organization is all over the place as well.

Try for one main font throughout and maybe a secondary font. Two primary colors are best with a third as a supplementary color. A shade of one of the two primary colors works well for the secondary color. Later in this chapter we'll look at website colors more closely to help you choose the ones that will work best for you.

Organization ought to be consistent. This means that the headers and footers should contain the same types of information. The inner pages should be organized the same across various sections. Each page's layout ought to be the same as well.

Navigation is another element that stays the same throughout the pages of great websites. Every page should have the same navigation elements in the same place. This conveys a sense of consistency and trust to your visitors.

Too often people feel lost while visiting a website. They may not know where they are or how to find what they're looking for. By offering consistent navigation you are giving users an anchor they can use wherever they are to find what they want. Also, since you teach the visitor to your home page how your organization and navigation works by simply presenting it to them, don't make them have to relearn a whole new system when they visit other pages within your site. This wastes their time and increases their frustration, which leads them away to your competitors' websites.

Easy-to-read content

Long, text-heavy and blocky paragraphs of unbroken text are not good. I really have to be into a topic or desperately need to glean the information to trudge through big chunks of unbroken text online. If I'm just shopping around for a product or service, you've lost me if I have to endure this kind of torture. Again, it is harder to read text on the Web than in other mediums such as books. Additionally, Web users are notoriously impatient, so make your content easy to read and non-intimidating. Use titles, sub-titles, small paragraphs, bullets, numbering and white space.

Any kind of frustration can drive your visitors to leave. By following Web conventions, you automatically make it easier to use. If something looks clickable, be sure it is actually a link.

Have you ever filled out a form, pressed the Submit button, and on the next page been asked to go back because you missed a field? When you go back does it frustrate you to have to figure out yourself which field you missed? Have you ever gone back to discover that all the fields you just spent a lot of time filling out were blank again and you had to start all over?

Don't do this to your site visitors. Web forms ought to include error validation. If you're asking visitors to enter their address and make the street a required field, the form should highlight the address field if it isn't filled out.

A good way to determine if your site is hard to use is by going through every feature of it yourself and seeing how easy it is for you. You could also ask other non-technical people to try using the features and ask for feedback.

Make sure your website is easy for your particular audience to use as well. For example, if your site attracts mainly retired people, avoid tiny text sizes.

Easily navigated and well organized

As I've already mentioned, if you present a navigational scheme on your home page, your users immediately start to learn where to find all the ways to locate elements of your site the minute they arrive. If you then place the same links in different spots on other pages you make it unnecessarily difficult for your viewers. It is annoying to users and gives the impression once again that you and your company are inconsistent and undependable. Don't make users work harder than necessary to get information from your site.

Not only should the navigation of your website be consistent throughout, but it should also be easy to use. People shouldn't have to hunt for links or for ways to move around your site. The organization of your site should be as simple as possible, make a lot of sense, and be well-represented by the navigation you present. In Chapter 8 I'll explain how to use flowcharts and story boarding to help you achieve this.

Provide a way for a user to get back to your home page on every page of your site. Often this is the page that is most familiar to the user. Make it easy to go back. If someone e-mails an associate a link to an inner page in your site and they click on it, it is a good idea to provide a way for that new user to get to your home page.

Clear navigation labels

Here are some examples of buttons that leave me dazed and confused:

A wedding site with a button called "Blanks"
A boating site with a button named "The Lighthouse"
A book site with a button labeled "The Inside Story"
A Web designer's site with a button for "Tea Time"

These sound more like Jeopardy categories than labels to more information. Imagine trying to find your way on the highway with signs reading "Over Here," "Moon Beams," "Lollipops." You'll need plenty of good luck to navigate your way through with those directions.

It's the same with navigating websites. Button and link names need to tell the visitor where the link leads. Make it as easy as possible for a visitor to know where they're going before they click. There *may* be times when naming a link an ambiguous name will pique the curiosity of a user and get the person to click on it. But as a general rule, keep your links and buttons as descriptive as possible.

Imagine sitting down at a restaurant and the waiter comes over to you and hands you five different menus, one for the appetizers, one for the soups and salads, one for the entrees, one for the desserts, and one for the drinks. Annoying. Now imagine if each menu had a different format, layout and method for listing the items. Brutal. I really don't want to work that hard at picking out my dinner. I'm hungry and just want a meal.

Don't make your Web visitors work hard by expecting them to re-learn your navigation system each time they enter another section of your site. They are hungry for useful information—and they're impatient.

When designing your navigation, keep in mind the cost-benefit analysis paradigm. When visitors are considering clicking on a link they are performing a quick cost-benefit analysis. Each time a person is presented with a link they haven't explored before, they try to determine whether the benefit they'll gain by clicking is worth the time and effort.

Don't underestimate this phenomenon. If you provide ambiguous, discouraging or repelling labels, people won't click. Remember, people are lazy and remorseless when deciding where to click next. Don't give them a reason for leaving your path.

A search function

Website visitors are purpose driven. They are visiting your site to find information or buy something. Make it as easy as possible for them to accomplish their goals.

A search function within your site is an excellent way to do this. If there is a specific bit of information that a person wants to find, don't make them wade through every page of your site. Implementing a search function is easy and free. You can get one at http://www.atomz.com/ and Google offers a free one through their AdSense program. This truly makes a site user's life a lot easier.

Quality, original content

Unchanging or outdated content is a sign of a lifeless website. People come back to a website to find new and useful content. And search engines rank you better when you are continually adding original content. Since there's so much information out there, my reasoning is there's got to be comparable information online that's more current. If you keep your content fresh your site will attract repeat visitors. And repeat visitors are more likely to turn into customers.

Well-written copy

Make every effort to have an error-free website. If there are careless mistakes made in spelling, grammar or punctuation, visitors may think you're careless in business and not trust you enough to buy from you. Mistakes erode trust. Copy ought to be specifically written for the Web. Don't just copy your print material onto your website.

User-oriented content and functionality

Generally speaking, no one cares about you, your company or your thoughts. What they do care about is what you can do for them. The characteristic is known as WIIFM (what's in it for me?). Sites that show pictures of the company building or tout their deep philosophy on the way business should be conducted really don't bode well for keeping the interest of site visitors. On the other hand, sites that speak directly to potential customers about how they can solve their problems, make their lives easier, safer, richer or more comfortable have a much better chance of keeping the eyeballs glued.

I get a chuckle from sites that devote a large section of their website to their executives. High-tech startups were once notorious for this. A typical section would have a long description of every executive, from the CEO to the CFO to all the various vice-presidents. They'd include photos of each person, and sometimes even include each person's pontifications on their business philosophy. This section would be prominently displayed on the home page with extensive links throughout the pages, all apparently appealing to the executives' egos but adding nothing to the company's bottom line.

No one cares. Your site visitors are there to get something accomplished, get information, sign up for something or buy a product. The website is not for you, it's for your visitors.

Text, not just images or buttons

Advertising agencies that also make Websites have a tendency to use too many graphics, often at the expense of text. A good rule of thumb is that if you have words in an image, take it out and replace it with HTML text. This is good for a number of reasons, including making the site more search engine friendly and loading faster. Search engines can only read key text, not words found in images. Also, graphic-intensive sites take longer to load.

If you don't include text versions of your links and only use buttons (which are images), then popular search engines can't index your site because they can't read links embedded in images. Always include text links as well as buttons.

Contact information

Don't make your Website an obstacle for your prospects and customers by neglecting to give your phone number. Every page should have your phone number listed. It is very frustrating to go to a company's site and have no way to reach them except through a form or e-mail.

Include your logo and tag line on every page as well. If you don't have a tag line, start thinking about creating one. Your site is a great place to repeatedly get your message out.

Technical Qualities

Here are some characteristics of a website that has excellent technical qualities. A technically superior site—

- Loads in browsers quickly

- Looks the same across platforms and browsers

- Has no broken links or images

- Never crashes

- Has form validation

- Interactivity works properly

- Does not require browser plug-ins to view properly

Create light pages that download fast

Since Web users are impatient, a page that takes too long to download or asks the visitor to go somewhere else to download new software just to view the site, he or she will simply leave. When I click on to a site and have to sit there waiting for it to appear in my browser, I know there are other sites out there with the same information that will download more quickly, so why wait? I'm gone. Optimize all your images so they have as small a file size as possible.

Looks the same across platforms and browsers

Three of the most popular personal computer platforms are PC, Macintosh and UNIX/Linux. PCs are the most popular, but people will viewing your site from all three platforms.

Internet Explorer, Firefox, Opera and Safari are all different browsers that people use. Internet Explorer is the most popular, but people will view your site with all of these browsers and more. Every platform and every browser renders websites a little differently. This means that your website will look a little different, depending on what platform and browser each visitor is using.

Making a website work and look the same with every browser is called "cross platform (or cross browser) compatibility." Be sure your site behaves and looks the same across all platforms and browsers and across the different combinations of these. Ask your Web vendor to test the site on all the platforms and browsers mentioned above.

Has no broken links or images

If your site has broken links, you look unprofessional and sloppy. You risk frustrating your visitors to the point where they will leave. You also make it harder for search engines to search and index your site. Images that are supposed to be present but show up as a broken image make your page look bad. Broken links and images means a broken website, which translates to visitors as a broken company.

Never Crashes

If a website's code is not written properly, the site may crash, meaning it will not work. If a site's server (see Hosting in Chapter 1) is not stable, or has hardware or software issues, the site will crash, meaning no one will be able to view it online until the problem is fixed. Sometimes a website won't work at all when using a specific platform such as Macintosh (see cross platform compatibility above). Make sure this doesn't happen to you. Test your site on all platforms.

Also be sure that your hosting company's server assigned to you can handle the load put on it by your website activity. For example, if you run a marketing campaign that you expect to generate a lot of website visitors, make sure your server has load balancing capability. You can find this out by calling your host provider and asking them. Load balancing means shifting extra activity that one server can't handle over to another server, balancing the load across more than one.

Sometimes a guest on a popular radio show will mention their website on air. Since I'm on the Internet all the time, I usually browse to their site, and half the time the site will not appear at all, instead giving me an error. This is because the people who run the website did not make sure the server where the website was hosted could handle a deluge of visitors all at once. What a waste.

I can picture the website owner pulling his hair out in frustration watching all those potential dollars evaporate. Load balancing could have solved this problem. I'll bet they would like to have read this before that happened.

Has form validation

Like I mentioned above, *a website's content should be easy to read, and the website's functionality should be easy to use.* All the forms on your website should have form error validation that makes the user's life easier. This means that each field in your Web form will have automatic validation to ensure that the user enters the correct information. If working properly, the form is programmed to tell users that they missed a required field or entered in words instead of numbers, for example. The better this works, the easier it is on the user. The more feedback that the form gives for entering incorrect information, the better it is for the user.

Good form validation also means you can ensure that you receive the information you want in the way that you want it. If your website will include one or more forms, ask your Web vendor to include good form validation. In the testing phase of site development (see Chapter 7) be sure to fill out the form using creative input to test if the validation works properly.

The interactivity works properly

One of the great things that any website has to offer its visitors is the ability to engage the user and allow them to take action. The Web is interactive, allowing users to steer themselves and choose the path they want to take. The more you allow users to interact with your site, the more engaging, memorable and attractive your site becomes. Web forms are a way to accomplish this. But other Web tools such as mortgage calculators, comparison mechanisms and product advisors based on input are also great examples of interactive elements.

Think of ways to engage your visitors so that they interact with your site in a way that helps them buy from you and keeps them coming. Of course, if you have functionality, be sure it works all the time, on all platforms and all browsers, no matter how many people use it.

Avoid plug-in requirements

If your website requires users to download special browser plug-ins to view your website properly, then you're going to lose a lot of visitors. An example of this is the Adobe® Flash™ player plug-in.

Flash is software that produces interactivity and animation. For a website that uses Flash, the browser that visitors use to view your website needs special add-on software (a "plug-in") to view your site. If they don't have the add-on, they'll need to go to the Adobe website and download and install it in their browser before they can proceed.

If you want to impress people with your bells and whistles, if you want to dazzle visitors with fast-moving graphics using Flash, then go ahead and require them to have the Flash plug-in or to obtain it if they don't. But if you want to make money with your site, do everything you can to make the lives of your visitors easy and simple.

Don't require them to have special software to view your site properly. Don't make them have to leave your site to download and install the correct software to view your website.

Marketing Qualities

- Attracts first-time visitors

- Is "sticky" (keeps the visitors from leaving)

- Impels people to return later

- Obtains new leads for you regularly by building your prospect e-mail list

- Converts visitors into customers at a high rate

- Builds your brand

- Evokes emotion

- Makes sales

- Has internal text links to all important pages

- Has a terms and policies page

- Has a phone number or other way to contact you

- Has your business tag line

- Is search engine optimized

People find websites using search engines more than with any other method. So it is vital that your website is search engine optimized, often abbreviated SEO. The two ways a site can be optimized for the search engines are on-page and off-page techniques, and both are equally important.

The more quality and relevant links that point to your website's home page and inner page, the better you'll rank, all other things being equal. Off-page optimization means getting links on other sites that point to your website. On-page optimization means including key words, phrases and semantically related words on your Website and in the source code

An expert SEO person or company will have experience in helping you achieve higher search engine rankings. To learn more about SEO, go to, "Search Engine Optimization (SEO)" beginning on 158.

Attracts first-time visitors

An important marketing quality that makes a website great is its ability to attract visitors to the site. This can be accomplished in a variety of very effective ways and will be discussed at length in Chapter 9. However, there are things that can be done to the site as it is being constructed that your Web vendor ought to know about and do. For example, every page in a website needs to be search engine optimized. This can be done as each page is built. (See the SEO section of Chapter 8 to learn more).

Another website element that can attract first-time visitors is good-quality, original, free content. Plan on including some of this in your business website. People often go online to gather information to help them make a purchasing decision. By offering visitors free content that they can't get anywhere else, quality content that is fresh and related to your business, you're establishing yourself as an authority. This attracts visitors.

Once a person learns of a great new resource he or she will tell other people. Some of these people will be website owners themselves and decide to link to you. Getting inbound links is vital for search engine rankings and will also give Web users a way to get to your site.

A "sticky" website

Getting people to visit the first time is less than half the battle. You'll need them to remain on the site long enough to take an action that benefits your business for the site to be effective. A site that gets people to stay there once they've arrived is called "sticky."

There are myriad ways a website can fail at stickiness. If the site fails to establish trust, people will probably leave. If the site seems shoddy, messy or unorganized, people will also leave. If the site asks too much of the user, like asking them to fill out a long form without offering any free teaser content before they can view valuable content, people are going to leave. If a site is confusing, people will leave. If a site has many broken links or "Page Not Found" errors, people are going to leave. This list goes on and on. By closely following this *Great Website Qualities* list, you'll avoid these problems.

On the other hand, if a website offers quality content that is original, you greatly increase your chances that a visitor will stay. If your copywriting is compelling, succinct and easy to consume, people will want to continue reading. You want people to stay so you can capitalize on their presence. For example, if your call to action is to get visitors to sign up for your newsletter, they'll need to be there long enough to accomplish the following:

1. Learn that there is a newsletter to sign up for in the first place

2. Begin to trust you as an authority in your industry

3. Get their interest piqued enough to want to learn more from you

4. Be compelled enough to actually sign up for your newsletter

5. Learn to trust you enough to feel comfortable with giving you their e-mail address

This works for selling online as well. As a matter of fact, it is even more important to establish interest, trust and authority to make a sale online because you are lacking the power of one-on-one in-person communication.

Another factor that makes a site sticky is its ease of use. People like to get maximum benefit for minimum effort. If they can achieve this while using your site, they'll linger.

Fresh content

Fresh and original content can help your website attract repeat visitors, since your visitors will keep looking for even fresher and more up-to-date content. If you provide it, they're more likely to keep coming back. If your website has solved a particular problem for a visitor in an easy and repeatable way, that visitor has a higher likelihood of returning.

Newsletters

Another website marketing element that gets people to return is newsletters that remind people that your website exists. Of course you'll need to capture e-mail addresses to do this. See below for a look at obtaining new leads.

New leads

Two common goals of business websites are to make sales and build a qualified prospect e-mail list. When services or products are difficult to sell online without the intervention of a sales person, a business website's main objective can be to build a list. Examples are complicated services that need in-depth explanations and hand-holding to get the sale. High-ticket items like automobiles are also hard to sell online. Car dealers should be building a prospect list by obtaining their website visitors' e-mail addresses.

Every website ought to be getting visitor e-mails. You spend a lot of time and effort building your site and even more time and money marketing it (see Chapter 9). Make sure you're trying to capitalize on every visit. Even if a website visitor doesn't buy anything from you on a first visit, if you get the e-mail address you'll be able to market to them in the future and make a sale later.

The goal is to send out relevant and anticipated e-mail newsletters to your ever-growing list. You have a form on your website that asks people to sign up for your e-mail newsletter. When someone signs up, they give you their name and e-mail address and receive a few automatic and customized e-mails that you can craft in advance. You'll need a database that stores each person's e-mail address and you'll need a way to send out regular e-mails to them all, including beautiful HTML newsletters (also called e-zines).

The benefits of this include the following:

- You are continually building a list of loyal readers that grows over time;

- Your readers spread the word that your organization is helpful, knowledgeable, and experienced;

- Your readers are regularly reminded of your organization's continued existence, growth and relevance, so they will return to your website;

- Some loyal readers will turn into loyal paying customers;

- You'll have a regular source of fresh and original content to add to your website which will help search engine rankings.

There are two distinct but equally important aspects of starting an e-mail newsletter that need to be addressed for you to accomplish the goals and gain the benefits listed above. First, you need the infrastructure and functionality to make all this happen, such as a database, an HTML form, and a method for sending out e-mails in quantity. Second, you need the content that will be in each newsletter.

Needed Infrastructure and Functionality for an e-mail Newsletter

You don't need to be technical to have the needed infrastructure for producing your own e-mail newsletter. A number of websites offer paid services that provide everything for you. The cost is a fraction of the cost of developing the infrastructure yourself. Two good examples of this type of service are "Constant Contact" and "Aweber."

Of course, you may already have something like this in place with your old website, or you may want to pay someone to develop it in-house so you can have it customized for your specific needs. You may integrate this into your existing contact management system, in which case you're going to need a programmer and a database administrator. But if you're starting from scratch and trying to save money, don't reinvent the wheel. Use an existing service.

Quality Content Needed for an e-mail Newsletter

It's not good enough to have infrastructure and functionality. You need content that makes people want to accept and read your newsletters over and over again.

Your newsletter ought to be related to your website and organization. Every person and organization has valuable and unique experience to offer others. And you'd be surprised at how many people want your unique knowledge. Sharing knowledge and experience with your current or future customers is what the Web is all about. People use the Web for getting information. Plan your newsletters around various aspects of your business or organization and make them educational so that your readers come away with more useful information than they had before.

Newsletters that are just extended advertisements don't cut it. If your newsletter consists of announcements of new or improved products or services, or specials that you're running, you're missing the boat completely. There is so much more you can offer.

You should aspire to creating newsletters that contain useful, relevant and anticipated information for your readers. You want to give away ideas and concepts for free that can be used to help improve some aspect of your readers' lives. You obviously don't want to give away the whole farm since a lot of your expertise is what you charge for in the first place. But giving some information away for free is a win-win.

Most often, your readers don't care about you or your company or your specific products or deals; they only care about what you can do for them. If they take the time to open your e-mail newsletter and read it, provide them with some real value or they won't bother again and your list will eventually wither away into oblivion.

In return for providing useful, original content, you will develop a constantly growing list of loyal readers who will spread the word that you are an authority in your field. Your readers may eventually buy from you if they haven't already

You can use your list occasionally to sell your products or services, but do this sparingly. You can also use the newsletter for selling advertisement space, but again, do this rarely. Finally, you can use your list to learn more about your customers and site visitors. You can ask the people on your list to fill out an online survey, but be sure to offer them an incentive for their time.

An internal customer e-mail list is a valuable asset for any organization. Handle it with loving care. Never sell or rent your list to anyone, try to offer value in your writing, and don't overuse it as an advertisement medium.

Converts visitors into customers

A high website conversion rate is a desirable feature for any business owner. By increasing the rate at which your visitors become customers, you don't need to increase your marketing efforts or budget. If you take the time to get people to come to your site, which you should do, then getting more of them to buy from you will follow. Conversions can also be applied to newsletter sign-up rates as well.

Many variables affect conversion rates. Headlines, copy, calls to action, the offer, price, urgency, button text, credibility seals such as Hacker Safe and BBBOnline, security assurances, and testimonials are examples. Every one of these can be tweaked to increase conversion rates. How can you do this? Try simple A/B testing where you offer half the visitors one page and the other half another page. Be sure to change only one variable at a time and test, test, test.

Builds your brand

Your website is an extension of your business. Ideally many people will visit it over its lifetime, so you want to make sure you are presenting a consistent company look that helps to build your brand. Be sure the look of your website matches your printed collateral materials such as brochures, letterhead or catalogs. Your site should also match your print advertising.

Even if you're a small business, building a brand is still important. You want people to recognize who you are without having to read anything. Be sure that your logo, colors, fonts, and style match across all your media. You should never have a website designed for you that looks different than the rest of your collateral materials or advertisements.

Evokes emotion

Marketing has everything to do with evoking emotion. The better your website evokes the right kind of emotion, the more money your site will make. Dry, dull and flat websites do nothing to move people. Sites that connect with the visitors always have a better chance of getting people to take action. Compelling copy can be a great way to awaken emotions in people. But a visual stimulus is even more powerful in arousing feelings that lead to sales.

Makes sales

Much of this book is dedicated to teaching you how to plan and create a site that makes as many sales as possible. The ability of an e-commerce site to make sale is an obvious quality that makes the site great. Marketing and sales are the fraternal twins of any company; the better your marketing, the better your sales.

Construct your website like a marketing machine. From the copy to the images, the layout to the navigation, the forms to the functionality and the links to the content, every single element in your business website needs to exist to help your visitors and market to them in a honest and effective way.

Has internal text links to all important pages

Search engines cannot find the inner pages of your site unless there is a text link somewhere else on your site pointing to it (unless other websites have text links pointing to your inner pages). In other words, unless there is a link on the Web somewhere pointing to a particular page, either on another website or on your own site, search engines cannot see that page.

For example, if you have a navigation bar with JavaScript drop-down menus pointing to your inner pages only, search engines like Google will not be able to find those inner pages. So it is very important that all of the pages on your site that you consider important have text links from other places on your site that point to them. Interactive navigation bars (like JavaScript menus) and images will simply not work.

An easy fix for this is to create a footer that contains simple text links that point to all your important pages, and repeat this footer on every page within your website. That way, all your pages are linking (pointing) to your important pages. You'll notice many websites do just this. Now you know the reason.

A Website Terms of Use and Privacy Policy

Again, building trust online is an important factor. One way to achieve this is to offer a Terms of Use and Privacy Policy that is accessible from every page. These documents should convey to the user that you are trustworthy and that you'll honor all promises made on your site.

Use these documents to tell your visitors explicitly what you do and do not do with any personal or contact information they give you. This is your chance to put your visitors at ease and show them that they can trust you. Have an attorney review your documents to make sure that you are not leaving yourself open to getting sued. By clearly stating what your terms and policies are, you can avoid most online problems.

Make it easy for people to reach you

Be sure to include a phone number or other way to contact you, including your business tag line under your logo

If you don't make it easy for people to contact you, they'll click away to a competitor. Don't use a website as a way to hide from your visitors. Instead, make it as easy as possible for them to learn how to contact you. Try to offer a phone number. At the very least, offer a few different e-mail addresses they can use to contact you or your employees.

As I mentioned earlier, the tag line and logo are important design qualities; they're also important from a marketing perspective. Use every page on your website as a branding opportunity. Include your logo and a brief tag line that communicates your main marketing message on every page.

Is search engine optimized

The best known search engine is Google, but other programs also use special software known as "spiders" to cruise the Web and build a database of data collected from websites. When visitors look for specific information, search engines point them to websites linked with key words from their database.

Far more people find websites with the help of search engines than in any other way. The development of on-page and off-page links to your site are a great way to optimize visits to your sites. The other way to search engine optimization (SEO)

is to provide key words or phrases on the Website and in the source code that the search engines will pick up.

An expert SEO person or company will have experience in helping you achieve a higher profile on the Web with accurate and relevant details about your website.

Ask for cross-platform tests

Make sure you ask your Web vendor to test the way your site looks across all browsers and platforms.

To learn more about SEO, go to "Search Engine Optimization (SEO)" beginning on page 158.

If your website has all the qualities listed on page 113, you are most likely achieving your site's goals and purpose. The more effective you are in accomplishing these things, the closer you will get to having a great site. I suggest that you copy the above list, edit it to fit your site's specific goals, and hand it to your Web vendor before they begin construction. They should use this as a guide for what you want.

One of the ways to define these subjective qualities is to research your industry and see what the standards are. Use the Web to conduct your research. Also, set benchmarks and then determine if you've achieved them.

For example, let's say that you are selling widgets online. Let's also say you've determined that average conversion rate in your industry for selling widgets online is five percent and that people search for widgets one million times a day. Among your website's goals is grabbing a larger and larger piece of those one million searchers, and having a conversion rate of at least five percent.

Imagine that the website's purpose is to make you so wealthy that you will be able to quit working. You define "wealthy" as a million dollars profit in five years. You then determine how many visitors you'll need to get five percent to buy your widgets so the profits will equal a million dollars in five years. For you to consider your site to be great, you need to accomplish this purpose. Anything less, and the site may be good, but not great.

You can do several things before you build your website and after it's completed to help ensure that it achieves your goals and purpose. First and foremost, as we have discussed at length in this book, is to hire the best and most appropriate Web design company or free-lancer you can. Be sure they understand your website's goals before they begin so they can build a site that matches your expectations as closely as possible. Also be sure to give them the "Business Website Rules" list and the "Great Website Qualities" list (See the Appendix, page 176) so they know what you expect.

You need to have a system in place so you can adjust the site as you learn what works and what doesn't. This needs to be planned in advance. Whether you decide to go back to your Web design company each time you want to make a change, pay the Web vendor to integrate a content management system where you or anyone else can change the site without the need for technical skills, or hire someone full time to do it for you, it's best that you plan for the need to make changes in your website after it's completed.

First, understand that all the "Great Website Qualities" are variable. By improving on them or tweaking them, you can get closer to achieving your website's goals and purpose. That's why it's important to

Prepare for change

Websites are not static entities. They ought to change and grow over time, so be sure to determine a way in which you can make regular website additions, changes and updates.

have an easy and reliable way to make changes to your website. For example, if you are trying to get more people to buy your widgets, then by improving your conversion rate, adjusting your headlines and copy will give you more sales. Making the home page and inner pages load more quickly could improve things as well.

Or let's say you are trying to get more people to sign up for your newsletter. You could increase your sign-up rate by adjusting the forms on your site and making them easier to use and quicker to fill out.

When you're in the planning phase of your new or re-vamped site, use the answers to your four questions in your Website Plan Document and the "Great Website Qualities" list to help you determine what you need to include and what you need to leave out. For example, if your goal is to create a new community for college students and you want to get as many members as possible, the look-and-feel of the site ought to be geared towards college-age people, and your written content ought to use their language.

Or if you are considering using Flash animation, ask yourself, "Will this increase my chances of achieving my stated goals?" If the answer is "Yes," then do it. If not, don't.

While you are in the process of managing the construction of your new or re-vamped website, be sure to employ focus groups. This does not need to be formal or involved. A focus group can be one person such as your mother or some other non-technical, older person.

Ask this non-technical person to try to use the first draft of the website's navigation. If she can figure out the site's organization with ease, most other people probably can, too. Or send a few of your friends the initial look-and-feel designs the Web vendor comes up with. Ask them for their subjective opinions. You may also ask your Web vendor to create two versions of a sign-up form for a few of your employees to test. Or you may want to use conversion testing on sales pages your Web vendor is creating. The more you determine before the website is finalized, the better off you'll be.

Of course, you'll want to explain to your Web vendor before they give you a final price quote that you plan on doing these things. It will most likely take up more of their time, so be sure to have this built into the contract and price before you begin.

Many of these elements can be included in an HTML template that is used for every page in your site. The template can include a link to your terms and policies. Templates make it easy to include site-wide elements and to quickly update or change them.

In your quest for building a great website, all of these factors need to be considered during the planning phase of the construction. You'd be surprised how many Web vendors are unaware of these important steps. How do I know this? It's obvious when I browse the Web. I am amazed at how many websites fall short. One way to beat your competition is to be sure to include all of these elements in your site.

In the appendix you'll find the Business Website Rules and the Great Website Qualities list. Print them out and include them among the things you send your Web vendor before they begin working on your new website.

By consistently putting yourself in the shoes of your website visitors you're sure to create a website that achieves your goals. When planning the architecture of your site, be sure that the flow of your site follows the rules I have just explained. When building a page, check to make sure each one consists of the qualities laid out above. To learn how to plan and implement your new website with your Web vendor, read on.

Chapter 8

Planning and Implementation

A Two-way Street with Your Vendor

The planning and implementation of your new website is a two-way street you travel with your Web vendor for the whole process. If you just give the vendor only a rough idea of what you want and then ask them to come back to you when they're done, expect that they won't come close to your original vision and that the Web pages they create for you won't meet your needs or successfully accomplish your goals.

This project should be one where you give a clear direction to the Web vendor at the start, and then provide constant feedback along the way to help guide the production of it to meet your original vision. Let them know that they'll need approval from you for everything they do, from the mock-up design to the final layout.

Only you know your business. Only you grasp the key nuances that set you apart from your competition. Only you know your audience. Only you have experience in your industry. If this is a new business for you and you're starting from scratch, it's up to you to learn these things before you begin your website planning phase.

The Web vendor doesn't care about learning the specifics of your business and industry. Most of them want to know some of these things to help them build a successful site, but you need to provide them with the information. If not, they'll charge you for the research, and the website will cost twice as much to build.

You have the Website Plan Document in your hand (explained in full in Chapter 3). In it you have the written goals of your new website. Remember, we're starting with the end in mind. You have your goals, and now you need to determine along with your Web vendor the best way to achieve them. By fully understanding your goals, your objectives and your strategies, you'll be better able to build a site that meets your requirements. Otherwise it's just a crap shoot. Ask questions such as:

- What type of site will accomplish these goals the best? (See Chapter 1 to understand the types of popular websites to choose from)

- Should we combine two types of sites? (For example, an e-commerce site that also has a blog and forum or an information site that has social-networking capabilities).

- What features does the site need to accomplish its business goals?

- What's the best way to organize the site to accomplish these goals?

- What needs to be included in the site to accomplish these goals?

- What Web strategies should we employ to meet the site's objectives?

- How has my competition done it and how can I improve on that?

Visual Structural Outline and Flow Chart

You'll need to work with your Web vendor to determine in advance exactly what the new website will contain, how it will be organized and how you want visitors to move through the site. You do this by creating a Visual Structural Outline and a Flow Chart. You visually represent the organization or architecture of the website in what I call a visual structural outline. And you visually represent the paths you want your visitors to take and how they get to where you want them to go in a flow chart.

A Website Visual Structural Outline

To begin work on the visual structural outline, use the rough website outline that you created as part of your Website Plan Document. This will help you determine the sections and pages that your new website needs to have in order to accomplish your goals. Just like when building a house, the builders have a blueprint to work from. They know exactly how many doors, windows, rooms and floors the house is going to have, and how all the pieces are organized. You need to be just as careful in your planning.

Your blueprint will be your visual structural outline. It doesn't need to be fancy. You could use actual visual structural outline software (sometimes called flow chart software such as Microsoft®'s Visio™) or you could sketch it on a piece of paper. If you choose the latter, be sure to do it in pencil because you will most likely want to change it many times before you're done.

Now would be a good time to sit down with the various people who have a vested interest in the site and learn what they need. If you have employees, co-workers or departments, be sure to ask them what their specific objectives are. Ask them what they want included in the website that will help them meet their specific needs within the business.

Keep in mind that every department usually thinks its job is the most important. Everyone wants a piece of the coveted home page space. They're all going to want the best features and include the best content for their part of the site. This is when diplomacy comes in handy. Keep the big picture in mind at all times. Don't get bogged down in website characteristics that have little to do with the website's main business goals.

The visual structural outline is going to be the representation of the architecture. For example, you may have five departments: Sales, Marketing, Product Development, Manufacturing and Support. Therefore, you may consider dividing the site up into five main sections that represent each of your departments. This is a common way to organize a website.

Suppose, however, you have an e-commerce store that simply drop ships. You don't have manufacturing or product development, and all your sales are made online. In this case you could organize your website around the types of people who purchase from you. Maybe your audience is divided up among scientists, small businesses and universities. You could divide your website up into three main sections with each section speaking directly to each of these three groups.

How you organize the site is determined by how you decide the site is going to achieve your pre-defined main objectives. Don't lose sight of this. You should come up with a rough draft of a visual structural outline with your co-workers or employees and then present it to your Web vendor to discuss how to make it happen. They may explain a better way to organize it to more effectively achieve your goals. In this case, listen to them carefully before you decide on a final draft. You may work with them and your department heads to determine the best organization together. The following diagram is an example of a website visual structural outline.

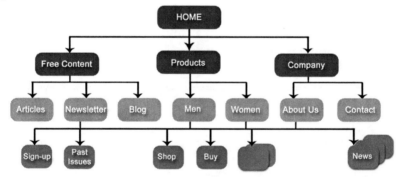

Figure 8.1 – A Visual Structural Outline

The visual structural outline represents the main navigation as well. If we are using the visual structural outline in Figure 8.1 the main navigation would include links or buttons called Free Content, Products and Company. Each of these would likely contain secondary navigation consisting of the sections in the second main row and so forth. We'll take a more in-depth look at navigation next.

However you decide to organize your website, map it out using a visual structural outline. This will help you determine what pages and sections are required and how they're organized.

A Website Flow Chart

A website flow chart is a visual representation of how site visitors accomplish their goals (which are your goals, too). Simply speaking, if your goal is to sell more widgets online, and your visitors go to your site to find and buy widgets, your goals are correctly aligned with your visitors' so that a flow chart will map out the paths they can take to accomplish this.

Check Website Rules and Qualities

If you find yourself having a difficult time deciding on a particular site structure or are arguing with your team, refer back to Chapter 7 and the Business Website Rules and Great Website Qualities lists to help guide your final decision.

For example, let's say you're planning on selling software through your website. Your goal is to get people to come to your home page, click through to a page that describes your software and the benefits, and click through to your purchase page.

See Figure 8.2 below for a visual representation of this flow.

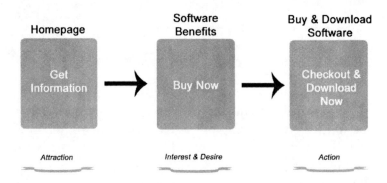

Figure 8.2 – A Simple Flow Chart

During the flow chart creation process, you utilize the AIDA test explained in Chapter 7. By forcing yourself to examine the common paths through your site, you can readily test if each step follows the attraction, interest, desire, and action

(AIDA) strategy. Notice at the bottom of Figure 8.2 that the AIDA is mapped out, too.

The home page ought to attract visitors and pique their interest enough for them to click on the "Get Information" link to the "Software Description and Benefits Page." This page ought to create enough desire to compel the visitor to click on the "Buy Now" link. The Purchase and Download Software Page ought to compel the visitor to take action, which would be to buy the software.

Not all visitors go to your home page

Keep in mind that although up to 50 percent of your visitors will come in through the home page, the rest will land on an inner page from a search engine or by following a link. Be sure that every single page offers them a call to action and a clear path to the goal.

Also, this is your chance to determine in advance how you want your visitors to go through your site. In other words, while you are developing the flow chart you can establish in advance how each visitor moves through a predetermined sales funnel that offers the highest likelihood of making them happy and getting the sale. Since your visitors may arrive at any page in your website, map this possible visitor path as well. It may be that they land on some random inner page. See Figure 8.3 for a slightly more complicated flow chart that incorporates the possibility of a visitor entering the site through an inner page.

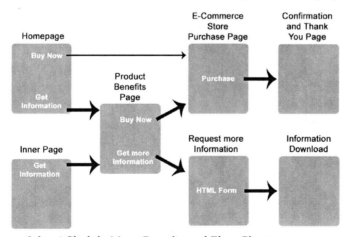

Figure 8.3 – A Slightly More Complicated Flow Chart

In Figure 8.3, notice that a visitor can enter the website by the home page or an inner page (which of course more closely resembles reality). If they enter via the home page then they have a choice to either "Buy Now" if they already know about your offerings, or "Get Information."

If they want more information, they click through to the "Product Benefits Page" (and you may have many of these pages). At this point, the visitor can either choose to click the "Buy Now" button or sign up for "More Information." If they choose "Purchase," they go through your e-commerce store checkout system by entering their credit card number and are finally brought to a "Purchase Confirmation" and "Thank You" page.

If they choose the other route of getting more information, they'll be brought to a "Request More Information" page, fill out a form with their contact information, allowing you to market to them in the future via e-mail, and then they'll be finally brought to a "Information Download" page. It's always a good idea to offer some kind of free incentive to visitors if you ask them to give you their contact information. See the Web Marketing section of Chapter 2 and Chapter 9 for more information on marketing and incentives.

Retail stores are set up in specific ways to steer customers through the store in order to maximize profits. (See the book, *Why We Buy*, by Paco Underhill to learn more about how stores do this and how you can apply the concepts online).

You need to come up with a flow that moves your visitors in such a way that they come closer and closer to buying from you. Make "Buy Now" buttons and links big. Be sure to present visitors with emotion-evoking images in key places where you believe they could be considering making a purchase. Most important, always include calls to action on every page.

Navigation

A key element you can use to guide people through your site is called navigation. The Web is interactive. As a visitor, you get to determine where you go and what you see. One of the most important features of every website is its navigation, and its navigation gives the controls to the visitor. Chapter 6 explained that you need to provide your Web vendor with a navigation scheme. Chapter 7 explained what qualities a great navigation system ought to include. Here we'll discuss how to organize it.

It bears repeating that every page ought to have the same navigation bar (a grouping of the main sections of your site). Don't make the user relearn the system when they get to a new page. Confusion drives visitors away. Consistency builds trust and facilitates finding what's desired.

I believe the navigation bar should be the same on every page including the home page. Since half your visitors will start on the home page, this is the perfect opportunity to introduce your site's structure as represented in the navigation bar.

Use the visual structural outline you made to create the navigation bar. Use the flow chart you made to determine how to best present the rest of the links to your visitors. The main sections which were mapped out in the visual structural outline become your navigation and the calls to action in your flow chart become the links that are specific to certain pages and aren't part of the main navigation bar.

There are many different types of navigation bars. They can be comprised of buttons, text links or JavaScripts. They can be horizontal under each page's main banner image. They can be vertical along the left or right sides of the screen. There can be more than one. For instance, you could have one navigation bar that points to all the main sections of the site run vertical and along the left side, and a horizontal one that runs across the top and points to all the company-related pages.

How should you organize your navigation bars? Ask yourself, What will make our visitors' lives the easiest, not make them spend needless time thinking things through, and help them best accomplish their goals?

Another good point is to stick to the *Clean, Simple, Easy* mantra. If a navigation bar is cluttered with 45 links on top of each other with no breaks, you're making visitors work too hard to find what they want. Finally, stick to Web conventions. Don't reinvent the wheel. You may have a designer who is dying to present your navigation bar in some weird but original way. Don't let it happen. You can't go wrong with a simple and small list of vertical links or buttons down the left hand side of each page. Since this is a standard, it's a sure bet.

Stay in the natural eye "path"

Eye-tracking studies have been done to determine where people's eyes move when they land on a Web page. They generally start from the top left an go to the middle of the page first. So be sure that your most important page elements, including your navigation, appear within this path. Now you know why so many websites place their logo in the top left. Even more importantly, always group your navigation in items of six or less. So if you have eighteen buttons in your vertical navigation bar, split them up into three visually distinct groups of six. Eye-tracking studies have shown that this works best for Web page viewers.

You may have a lot of pages that you want represented in the main navigation bar. In this case, employ roll-over menus. This is usually done with JavaScript. Here's how that works. If you refer back to Figure 8.1, you can see that the main naviga-tion may only have three visible links when you land on the page: the "Free Content," "Products," and "Com-pany" links. JavaScript lets you offer function-ality to a visitor that allows them roll his mouse over any one of these three, causing a new sub-menu to pop out that shows the sections contained within.

See Figure 8.4 for an example of a main navigation bar button called "Support" that produces a sub-menu when rolled over.

Remember the Great Website Qualities list in Chapter 7 of the technical aspects of a website? One of the key elements is functionality that works across all popular platforms and brows-ers. This extends to navigation as well.

If you include roll-over menus in your navigation, be sure the roll-over functionality works for everyone, regardless of the platform or browser they're using. JavaScript is supported by all popular browsers, which is why I suggest using it, but you still need to test it using various platforms and browsers to be sure your navigation tools work for everyone.

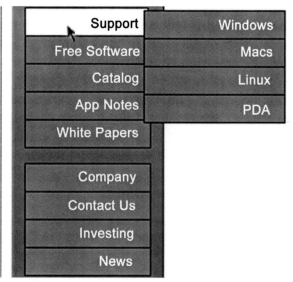

Figure 8.4 – Sample Navigation Bar

When deciding on your navigation bar structure, think in terms of how your visitors see and use the site. To do this, try to group similar sections from the point of view of the user and what the user will want to do. Support sections should be grouped, and company sections should be in a separate grouping. See Figure 8.3 for an example.

If users want to go to your site to find the answer to a question regarding the hardware or software they've purchased from you, they will scan the navigation bar and find the top grouping of support links easily. But if another user is interested in learning more about the company to possibly invest in it, they'll find and use the second grouping more easily if the two groups are clearly separated.

Choosing the Right Website Colors

If you already have an established brand and logo or existing collateral material, be sure to stick with the colors you've been using. You want to make sure that your brand and your

147

company's appearance is the same across all marketing media, including the website.

If you are creating a brand new website, you face the challenge of deciding on the right color scheme for your site.

Color is often overlooked in the business of optimizing websites for a better return on investment. Few business owners know that Website sales can be affected significantly by simply changing the colors. If you ever want to experience an eye-twisting headache, try reading yellow print on a blue background or any website that uses some funky combination of print and background colors. The reason you see black type on a white background so much is that it is the best color combination for readability both online and off.

Color	Positive Connotations	Negative Connotations
Red	Sense of power, strength, passion, sexuality	Anger, forcefulness, impulsiveness, impatience, intimidation, conquest, violence and revenge
Yellow	Caution, brightness, intelligence, joy, organization, spring time	Criticism, laziness, or cynicism
Blue	Tranquility, love, acceptance, patience, understanding, cooperation, comfort, loyalty and security	Fear, coldness, passivity and depression
Orange	Steadfastness, courage, confidence, friendliness, and cheerfulness, warmth, excitement, and energy	Ignorance, inferiority, sluggishness and superiority
Purple	Royalty, sophistication, religion	Bruised, injured, foreboding
Green	Money, health, food, nature, hope, growth, freshness, soothing, sharing, and responsiveness	Envy, greed, constriction, guilt, jealousy and disorder
White	Pure, fresh, easy; cleanliness or goodness	Blind, winter, cold, distant

Since it is even harder to read text on a monitor than it is on paper, we must be especially careful with the colors we choose for our websites, or we will suffer less-than-optimal site traffic and fewer repeat visitors.

Color choice should also be dictated by subtleties in human psychology. Different colors invoke different emotions, are associated with specific concepts, and say different things to people in each society.

For instance, green is often associated with freshness or money, which is fairly obvious if you think about it. Every color has standard associations, although some of the emotions and concepts are subtle. In our culture, white means pure, easy, or good, and purple can be associated with royalty or sophistication. In China, white is the color for funerals, and in Brazil purple represents death.

What's more, each color carries with it both positive and negative connotations. The emotions and concepts that you associate with specific colors may differ from other people's, but themes run throughout each color. Here are some colors and associated emotions based on mainstream American culture:

A major goal of marketers is to invoke emotion in their audience. We know that if we can cause some kind of an emotional reaction in the people we are marketing to and communicating with, we have a better chance of compelling them to buy from us. The battle between logic and emotion that rages in each of us is won by emotion most of the time. By choosing the colors of our websites and online media with deliberate care, we purposefully invoke a specific emotional response that will increase sales. Pick your colors carefully.

When I am not sure exactly which colors or combinations to use, I often start trying different things, then take a step back and ask myself what my chosen colors are conveying to me.

Since website visitors all have different platforms, different monitors, and different settings for their screen resolutions, the colors you choose for your website may not always be rendered in exactly the same way on your site visitors' monitors.

That's why there are "Web Safe" colors that have a much higher likelihood of looking the same regardless of the user's computer, monitor or settings. Many graphics programs, including Adobe Photoshop, have a feature that allows you to choose "Web Safe" colors only. Be sure to ask your Web vendor to use Web safe colors only.

Your color choice is vital. Be sure to try different colors, shades, contrasts and combinations before you decide. Work with your Web vendor to determine what looks best.

It's a lot of fun playing with colors, but since every choice you make comes with a set of pre-defined societal meanings and emotions, choose with deliberate care.

Mock-ups

Using all the materials we've presented, your Web vendor is now poised to begin work. They understand your future website's goals, objectives and strategies. They have your Website Plan Document, which gives them a brief outline of the site. They have your website's visual structural outline and flow chart that gives them an in-depth map of your future website. They know how the navigation is going to be structured and they know the colors and fonts you want to use. You've provided them with everything I suggested in Chapter 6 and they're ready to go.

The next step is to expect a rough black and white mock-up of the home page and a typical inner page from your Web vendor. Use black and white mock-ups first so you can truly see the layout and page flow without getting distracted by colors.

Expect them to make mock-ups as images first, not in HTML because it is easier and quicker to create a large, non-functional, static image of a Web page instead of coding the whole thing in HTML. If you need changes made based on what you see in a mock-up, they can be made much more easily in an image. This saves you time and money.

Every page needs to have certain elements and should have an effective layout. So when you're looking at the mock-ups presented to you, be sure to check these things:

- Is there a clear visual hierarchy on the page? Is there a page header that effectively describes the whole page and is it obvious? Are the subheadings over their respective sections on the page? Does the page follow Web conventions? (Web conventions are mostly borrowed from print conventions, so if you've ever read a magazine or newspaper, you'll know what to expect on your Web page.)

- Is there an effective use of white space? Remember our *Clean, Simple, Easy* mantra? Cluttered, busy and complicated pages force visitors to puzzle things out. We don't want that. Busy pages confuse users. They make it hard for them to accomplish their goals. The effective use of white space helps clean things up.

- Is there an obvious call to action on the page? Does the page follow your flow chart which should purposefully move your visitors through the site the way you want?

- Is the navigation bar organized the way you determined in advance? Is it easy to use? Does the navigation precisely follow your visual structural diagram? Does it follow basic Web conventions?

- When referring back to your Great Website Qualities list, does the page follow the effective design qualities? For instance, is the text broken up into small, readable chunks? Are the links or buttons in the navigation properly and unambiguously labeled? Is your logo prominently displayed?

Once you've found the perfect mock-up that best represents the vision for the website, establish a *design freeze*. Ask the Web vendor to make the changes and present you with an updated version. This process may take a few iterations, but be patient; it's worth it to get it right. Eventually, and hopefully not in too much time, you'll be presented with a version that's perfect for you

The next step is for them to present you with the color version of the mock-up. Here you'll evaluate the colors to make sure they match and convey the right message. Ask them to post the color version of the mock-up to the Web, either on their servers or in a hidden place on your server.

This way you'll be able to see exactly how the colors are rendered by your computer and any other computer you use to view it. If changes are needed, go through the same iteration process as you did with the black-and-white mock-up creation. The next step is for the Web vendor to recreate the color mock-up in HTML. Sometimes there are issues going from an image to a functional HTML page. HTML has constraints; it's the nature of the beast. Browsers are also limited in the way they can present content. So there are times that a mock-up presented as a graphic cannot be perfectly mirrored when developed in HTML. This part of the phase catches these issues which in turn will help you figure out what to do if the problem arises.

Again, ask them to post the HTML page to a server for you to view it on the Internet. This will reveal to you exactly how it's going to look to your visitors.

Don't embed text in images

Once you begin the HTML mock-up phase, be sure that almost all of the text on the page is text and not embedded in images. Pure design companies are notorious for creating websites that contain mostly images (because designers have much more flexibility when designing images that aren't limited by HTML constraints.) They'll often embed most or all of the text within the images, which means that the search engines have nothing to read when visiting your site. By not having actual text on your site you'll be invisible to search engines. Engines simply can't read text within images.

If there are others in your organization who have a say in the development of the website, now's the time to show them the color HTML mock-ups. Be sure to get them to agree with the final mock-up that you choose.

Once you've found the perfect mock-up that best represents the vision for the website, establish a a design freeze. Now that you and your bosses, employees or co-workers have agreed on a final version, no more changes can be made. This is vital, especially if you are working with other people in your company.

At this point your Web vendor ought to begin coding the rest of the site in HTML. This can be time consuming. If halfway through this process you or someone else in your organization decides that they like green better than blue, then you just paid the Web vendor to develop pages that you will no longer use. They'll have to start all over and charge you for the new work.

Or your marketing department may want the navigation bar to be along the top instead of down the side. Again, if the Web vendor has developed ten pages in HTML, it's going to be time consuming and costly to do them all over. So stick to the design freeze once everyone's agreed on the final layout.

Putting it All Together, Testing and Going Live

By now, the Web vendor has a color HTML mock-up that you have approved. A design freeze is in place. The mock-up can now be used as a template for the rest of the site. They should also have all your content in hand. Their next step is to begin work inserting the content into the template.

As each section of the website is created in HTML by the Web vendor, ask them to post all the pages that make up each section, with working links, to a private server for your review. Don't let them go back to their offices and create the entire site without your reviewing it along the way. You'll be able to catch all kinds of little things that need changing before they replicate the problem or issue across the entire site.

When they finish the first section, have them post it to the Internet in some place where only you can view it. Go over it with the eye of a site visitor. Is the layout easy to read? Does it follow all the Business Website Rules? Does it contain the qualities from the Great Website Qualities list? Is it clear to you how to navigate effectively? Are there mistakes in spelling or grammar? Does the functionality work easily and properly? Ask a few other non-technical people who are not in your business to review it as well and record their feedback. Then compile a list of any issues or problems you find into one document (an e-mail or Word) and give it to the Web vendor to fix before they go on to the next section. Repeat this process with each section until the site is complete.

When the whole site has been announced complete by your Web vendor, use the same tactics to review everything. Ask them to post the site to the Internet on a testing server so you, your employees, your boss, or your co-workers can review it. Ask people who are not in your industry to review it as well.

Test everything. Test all the links. Test the functionality of any interactive features. Have a good writer review the copy for spelling, punctuation and grammar mistakes. Review the site on a Macintosh computer and a PC. View the site using Firefox and Internet Explorer browsers. Compile a list of all feedback and issues you've found and send it to the Web vendor in one complete document for them to address. When they're done, ask them to post it live to your hosting provider server again.

You'll probably need to give information for logging in to your host provider in order for them to do this. Be sure that they hook up your host provider's server to your domain name (this is called setting the DNS).

Voila! You now have a great production website that's live on the Internet. After all this work, you'd think you could take a break. But as I explained in Chapter 2, the third pillar of a website is marketing. Just because the site is on the Web does not mean that anyone will find it. You still have one more important and ongoing step to take to ensure that all this effort was worthwhile.

Chapter 9

After It's Built, You HAVE to Market It

How to Build Revenues Through Smart Marketing

A colossal mistake people often make after their website has been built is assuming that if they build it, people will automatically come. This is not true.

Think of your website as a brand-new brick and mortar store in the middle of the Amazon rain forest. No one, and I mean no one, is going to find that store. (Well, maybe a wandering aborigine or two, but they probably won't have credit cards or U.S. currency.)

You must plan on getting the word out about your site. If it was a re-vamp of an existing website, you may already have existing traffic, but you'll probably need more to offset the cost of re-building it. If this is a brand-new website, plan on implementing a Web marketing campaign to drive qualified traffic to your new site; otherwise the site will rot alone.

You may tackle this subject yourself or assign it to an employee, or you may ask your Web vendor to do it. If you want your Web vendor to do it, consider asking them to include it in the project proposal before you sign the contract.

That way, you may get a discount for bundling services from one company. Beware: many Web design firms are not expert online marketers. Utilize some of the techniques described in this book to determine their expertise.

Ask them for references from clients for whom they've done Web marketing or, as it is sometimes called, "e-marketing." Ask them to provide numbers showing increased traffic resulting from their marketing efforts. In other words, you should find out how much monthly traffic their clients had before they marketed the site, and how much the monthly increase was after they did a campaign.

Ask for website statistics from their server logs. The Internet is full of unscrupulous salesmen masquerading as Web marketing gurus and experts, so be especially careful who you hire and who you give your money to. Hire a reputable Web marketing company—preferably the Web vendor you hired to build your site in the first place—that can create and manage an integrated online marketing campaign for you over a period of time.

Finding a marketing vendor

If you decide to use a different vendor for your Web marketing work, you can use the same techniques explained in this book to find a Web design firm. Refer back to the chapters in Section 2 – "How to Hire a Web Designer or Company" and utilize the same methods, but this time search for an e-marketing vendor.

Internet marketing is such an involved subject that an entire book could be written about it, and many have been. This book has been mainly about hiring a Web vendor to re-vamp an old site or how to get online for the first time. We have also talked about making a new website successful in business, and e-marketing is an integral part of that.

Web marketing is crucial to any website or online business. You need website visitors or your site is useless. The only way to obtain traffic is to market your site. Generally speaking, the more traffic your site gets, the more money your site makes. Fortunately, there are a wide range of various e-marketing techniques to choose from. Online marketing is rich in opportunity, and no concept is too difficult to learn and eventually implement.

It is worth your while to investigate all the ways in which you can market your website online once it's live. In this chapter you will learn the possibilities. Also, remember that Web marketing is dynamic. The techniques and the industry are constantly changing and evolving. What I describe here is a snapshot for the current top methods (2008). Different and better ways will surely come about, and soon.

Even in the turbulence of constant change, e-marketing principles will remain the same. In the Web Marketing section of Chapter 2, I explained these fundamental e-marketing principles. Here they are again, slightly modified:

E-Marketing Principles

Marketing continues

Web marketing is not a one-time affair. To truly get the most of your website (which in the business world means getting the most profits), you must commit to ongoing or at least periodic e-marketing campaigns

- Give Web travelers a reason to visit your site.

- Don't assume that others care about you, your business or your website; all they care about is what your business, through your website, can do for them.

- Don't expect anything—contact information, for example—from visitors unless you give them something in return.

- Emotions are the strongest motivators.

- One-to-one marketing thrives on the Web.

- Interactivity is the nature of the Web. This makes it easy to have a dialog with your visitors about their thoughts, their needs, and what you'd like to know about them. This, in turn, allows you to identify their needs more accurately and respond appropriately.

- An e-marketing program is always dynamic. As data come in about the success or failure of the program, adjustments need to be made for continual improvement.

- Analyze the data your Website produces to give you immediate feedback about the success of your e-marketing initiatives. Server Web log files and website analytics programs such as Google Analytics or WebTrends can help you analyze your website's activity.

- Driving traffic to a site is not enough. Traffic needs to be converted into paying customers.

- Give people the useful, free and relevant information they crave online, and they will be more loyal to you.

- The less your touting of your company, product or service competes with the useful information you're offering, the more people will trust you and be loyal to you.

The most common and effective types of online marketing are the following:

- Search engine optimization

- Pay-per-click (paid search advertising)

- Link building

- Article marketing

- Web 2.0 and social bookmarking

- E-mail marketing

- Affiliate marketing

- Video marketing

Search Engine Optimization (SEO)

By far, most people find websites using search engines. Search Engine Optimization involves on-page and off-page development. The on-page development

Beware of anyone who claims they can guarantee top search engine placement. Unless they actually work for Google or Yahoo, they can't guarantee anything.

encompasses reworking the visible content and behind-the-scenes HTML code on a Web page to show up higher in the search engine ranking positions (SERPs). The off-page work involves building links on other, relevant websites that point back to your Web page. These types of links are called inbound links. In general, the more relevant your inbound links are, and the larger number of inbound links you have, the higher you rank. This is an oversimplification, but gives you an idea what you're aiming for. There are hundreds of ways to do both of these things, and an expert SEO person or company will have experience in many of those ways.

The three main search engines today are Google, Yahoo and MSN. Google is the king of engines today, making up a larger market share than both Yahoo and MSN combined. The other search engines besides these three are basically irrelevant. So beware of services that offer to submit your site to thousands of search engines, that won't do a thing.

To check if a company is actually successful at search engine optimization, go to Google and type in various search terms to attempt to find their company website. Use longer keyword phrases such as the services they provide along with the city they are in. If they don't show up anywhere, maybe they are not that good. Also, ask them for search phrases that can be used to find their company website or their previous clients' websites. They ought to show up on the first or second page to consider them successful. Ask them to provide client websites and keyword phrases they have optimized for and look those up too.

Tips for the SEO Newbie

Here are some tips that should help even the newest website owner understand the key points in helping search engines find your site:

1. Be sure that every page on your site has a unique title tag and meta description tag that contains the keywords you want that page to rank for. These tags are HTML that go at the top of every Web page in the source code.

If you don't know what these tags are, be sure to talk about this with your Web vendor. They will definitely know what they are, but may not be aware that they are crucial in ranking well in search engines.

Let's say your website sells blue widgets, among other items. If so, then the page on your site that talks about blue widgets should have a title and description tag that look something like this:

<title>Buy Blue Widgets</title>

<meta name= "description" content="If you are looking for affordable blue widgets, shop here.">

Notice how I use the keyword phrase, "blue widgets," in both tags? You should do the same for every page on your site, and every page ought to have unique title and description tags.

2. Be sure to have a footer section on every page of your site that contains text links pointing to other important pages on your site. They need to be text links and not images, rollover buttons or interactive navigation menus. Search engines can only follow text links. Using our blue widgets example, you ought to include a text link that says "blue widgets" in the footer of your home page and all other pages that point to your blue widgets page.

3. Go out onto the Web and find places where you can get links that point back to your blue widgets page. For example, you may leave a comment in a blue widgets-related blog that says something like, "I found a website that offers discounts on blue widgets. Check it out." Here you would make the words, "blue widgets," the link that points back to your blue widgets page. Or you may ask people you know who own websites to add a link to your blue widgets page as well. There are

hundreds of other ways to acquire links to your pages, I suggest doing a search on Google for something like "link building strategies" or "how to build links" or "link building tips." If you choose to leave comments on blogs or use Web 2.0 website to build links back to your website, be sure you are adding to the conversation with valuable remarks. Don't just try to build links for the sake of building links. Rather, contribute in some valuable way to the blog or site with unique ideas.

4. The words that are the links (underlined and blue) are the words that search engines use to determine rankings. In other words, if you go out there and build links to your website, but every link is the name of your company, then you'll rank well for your company name. If you want to rank well for blue widgets, then you need to create links with the text that says blue widgets. This is the way a link is constructed with blue widgets as the text: <a href="http://www.mysite.com">blue widgets</a>

5. Be sure to use the phrase "blue widgets" often on your blue widgets page. It should be in the header tags (ask your Web vendor about header tags), it should appear in the first and last paragraphs and maybe should be bolded a few times. Finally, include words that are related to blue widgets on the page. This is called Latent Semantic Indexing (LSI). Search engines use the words around a phrase to better determine the page's relevancy to that phrase. Latent Semantic Indexing allows a search engine to determine if you're talking about the instrument or the fish when using the word "bass." So if you want to be found for the phrase "bass fishing," use related words on the page such as boat, fishing pole and lakes.

Pay-Per-Click (paid search engine marketing)

When you do a search and arrive at a page of links and descriptions in the search engine's results, you'll probably find a column on the right hand side of the page that includes other links and descriptions to websites. These are called AdWords on Google, YPN on Yahoo and Live Search Advertising on MSN. They are all forms of pay-per-click advertising.

Google explains its AdWords service like this:

When people search on Google using one of your keywords, your ad may appear next to the search results. Now you're advertising to an audience that's already interested in you. You're charged only if someone clicks your ad, not merely when your ad is displayed. You can, for instance, set a daily budget of five dollars and a maximum cost of ten cents for each click on your ad.

The payment for each click is calculated using a bidding system. The higher you bid, the higher your ad will appear in the results. This is an excellent way to advertise your website. Think of pay-per-click like the Internet age's answer to newspaper classifieds. Of course they are much better because you're reaching more people and the people you reach are targeted, meaning they are already interested in your subject.

Some companies have built entire business models using only this Web marketing technique. It can be that effective. And you can spend a lot. I know of companies that spend hundreds of thousands of dollars a month for this service alone. (Now you can see why Google's stock is so high!) Since it can cost so much, consider hiring someone to monitor your pay-per-click campaigns on a regular basis. You could assign that task to an existing employee or outsource it.

Link Building

Attracting more links to your website, or "link building," has two benefits. First it gives your website another way to be found besides search engines. Although search engines are the main way people discover websites, following links from other websites is also common.

Think about how many times you found a new site (or recognized a site you've already been to) by clicking on a link. Any site that is relevant to your website's topic is a potential place to create a link. Even if your site doesn't rank well in Google and you have no budget for pay-per-click advertising, you will still get website traffic from links directing traffic to you from other sites.

The second benefit of link building is its effect on your website's search engine rankings. As mentioned above, a significant amount of the ranking algorithm for Google and other search engines consists of off-page factors—in other words, links. The more relevant websites that link to your site, the higher your rankings will be (all other things being equal). And links from highly trusted websites (called authority sites) count even more. Good links are a mixture of quantity, quality and relevancy. There are many ways to get links, but this topic is beyond the scope of this book.

In Chapter 7, "What Makes a Website Great," I suggested that one key quality of a great website is high-quality, fresh and original content. Not only does good content make your site better and offer more value to your visitors, but it also acts as a magnet for inbound links. Probably the number one way in which you can build links to your website is to regularly write and add new and original content to your website. This will attract more people and cause some of those people to link to your website because they like the content.

Two other common ways to build links are article marketing and Web 2.0 utilization. See below for their descriptions. Also, consider using these search phrases in your favorite engine to find tutorials and articles that explain link building strategies more fully:

- Link bait

- Link trading

- Purchase links

- Article on link building

- How to build links

- Directory lists

- How to syndicate through RSS

Go to Google and download their search tool bar. Included in it is a green Page Rank bar, which is Google's measure of the importance of a page. The more green you see when visiting a site, the higher its Page Rank, and the better Google judges the site as a source of a link to your website.

The worst kind of link building is sending unsolicited e-mails to Web masters asking for a reciprocal link. Your message will be as welcome as a mosquito bite. On the Web bad or unscrupulous methods of communicating are called "spam." Do not use these. Look up "what is link spam" in Google to get a better understanding of what to avoid.

Article Marketing

Article marketing serves two purposes. Since content is king, articles are a great way of providing new content for your site. When you write original articles (or pay someone to write them for you) you are creating fresh content to post on your site. Of course the article topics need to be relevant to your website. This is article writing's first purpose.

The second purpose article marketing serves is link building. You can post your articles on other people's websites. Because original content is so highly regarded on the Web, many people are looking for new content to add to their sites. Provide them with your articles. At the end of each of your articles include an author by-line. This is a sentence or two that explains who you are or what your company does, and includes a link back to your website.

If you write an article and submit it to ten websites, and each has your by-line at the end and includes a link pointing back to your website, you've just created ten new links. Since Google may not give you ten links worth of credit if the article is the same (duplicate content), consider writing ten different versions to get the most bang for your buck. You can also use article spinning software to make each version unique.

Using your favorite search engine, you can find many article writing and site submission services.

Web 2.0 and Social Bookmarking

Web 2.0 is a new generation of websites that take user-contributed content to the next level. It consists of blogs, social bookmarking websites, and user-generated websites on the new generation of the Web. Combined, these sites reach a large readership. Social bookmarking sites provide users with a place to store, categorize, annotate and share favorite Web pages and files. See Chapter 1, "Websites and What They're Made Of," for a full description of Web 2.0 and examples.

You can utilize Web 2.0 websites by getting your site bookmarked, referenced or talked about on other sites. A healthy number of people who come across these references will visit your site. Web 2.0 sites are a form of link building. There may be a time when quality references in Web 2.0 sites will be figured into search engine rankings as well. Or this time may already have arrived.

Here are three examples of Web 2.0 sites and how to use them:

YouTube: Create a video that mentions your website and upload it to YouTube and when people watch your video, they may be moved to visit your website.

Digg: Write an original article (or pay someone to write an article for you) and upload the title, description and link to Digg.com. People vote on your article, pushing the good ones to the top of the list. When people search the Digg site and come across your article, they'll click through to your website to read the full text.

Technorati: Create a blog, video or photo and upload it to Technorati. Technorati defines itself as follows:

> Technorati is the recognized authority on what's happening on the World Live Web, right now. The Live Web is the dynamic and always-updating portion of the Web. We search, surface, and organize blogs and the other forms of independent, user-generated content (photos, videos, voting, etc.) increasingly referred to as "citizen media."

Just like with our other examples, when people go to Technorati and find your content in a search, they will likely visit your website.

E-mail Marketing

> **Unsolicited e-mail is spam**
>
> Never send e-mails to people who have not opted-in to receive e-mails specifically from you. Otherwise you'll be sending unsolicited e-mails, a.k.a. spam, which has given e-mail marketing a bad name and made it somewhat controversial. Stay away from that problem.

E-mail marketing is as old as the Internet. It remains somewhat controversial, but is still effective. E-mail marketing involves sending e-mails to people in an effort to get them to click through to your website and take some kind of action.

You can rent opt-in e-mail lists from e-mail brokers, craft an e-mail message, either in plain text or HTML, and include in the message an offer and link. You then send the e-mail to the rented list, and expect a small percentage to click on the link in the message and take you up on your offer. The offer could be to buy your product or to sign up for your newsletter, for example. E-mail selling is the online equivalent to direct mail marketing. In both direct e-mail and mail marketing, a response rate of one to three percent is considered acceptable.

Another form of e-mail marketing is sending e-mails to your own house list (as opposed to a rented e-mail list from a broker). In this case, over time you compile a list of e-mails that you store in a database and periodically send e-mail messages to. This list will most likely come from your website form's such as a "Contact Us" form, or a newsletter sign-up.

The online newsletter, or e-zine, has become a popular and effective marketing tool and communication medium for website owners as well. Most often, there is a simple sign-up form on a website that asks for the visitor's name and e-mail address and offers a free digital newsletter that will be sent out periodically.

The more useful and unbiased the information, the more people sign up for the newsletter and read it. In other words, if all you send out is an advertisement each time, people will not find it useful. However, if you send out industry news, articles, tutorials and relevant information to help them in their life or their work, people will look forward to receiving and reading the newsletter. Remember, people don't care about you, they only care about themselves and, possibly, how you can help them.

Some companies and individuals make their entire income using e-mail marketing. Many websites have the goal of acquiring as many e-mail addresses of site visitors as possible because they believe that a site visitor is lost forever if they don't at least get their e-mail address. They are also persuaded that spending money and effort trying to increase website traffic without obtaining an e-mail address is a waste.

Affiliate Marketing

Wikipedia's definition of affiliate marketing is as follows:

Affiliate marketing is a method of promoting Web businesses (merchants/advertisers) in which an affiliate (publisher) is rewarded for every visitor, subscriber, customer, and/or sale provided through his/her efforts.

Amazon.com was one of the Web's first big affiliate marketers, and some say this technique saved their company during the dot com bubble burst.

Affiliate marketing is simple. Amazon, for example, pays website owners to include a link to relevant books. If a site visitor clicks on an Amazon.com book link and ends up buying it, Amazon pays them a commission. Whenever you see an Amazon.com logo on a website you're visiting, chances are it's an affiliate link.

This concept can be found everywhere on the Web today. If you have a product, you can create an affiliate program. This program encourages others to sell your product as long as you give them a cut of the revenue. This can create an army of "salespeople" for you and greatly extend your reach. Examples of affiliate programs are ClickBank, Commission Junction, LinkShare, FusionQuest or Affiliate Tracking Network. You can find many other programs to include your product in by searching affiliate directories and conducting searches online.

Video Marketing

A more recent form of online marketing is the direct result of generally available higher bandwidth. Since more people today have high speed connections, watching video online is easy. Video marketing is related to Web 2.0 in that you can create a video to promote your business and then upload it to numerous video-sharing website communities. Of course the big one is YouTube, but there are many others as well.

Video marketing extends beyond Web 2.0. Since it's relatively easy for any amateur with a digital video recorder to shoot a video, and there is a lot of software that can help anyone edit it and make it Web-ready, creating videos has never been easier.

Here are some ways you can use videos in marketing your website and business:

- Introduce yourself and your company to your website visitors. Tell about your services. Build trust.

- Explain and demonstrate in front of the camera how to use your product.

- Prepare an online sales letter that explains the features or benefits of your product or service.

- Offer an online video as a bonus for purchasing another product of yours.

- Enhance your product pages with videos for a more effective way to deliver your marketing messages.

Video marketing will most likely become more and more common as bandwidth opportunities increase, and connections become cheaper. People seem to respond better to video than to text or audio alone, so it really is a marketer's dream.

Website analytics

Another excellent aspect of Web marketing is the ability to track the success of each effort. Never before in marketing has it been so easy to accurately see what your actions are producing. In the old days a newspaper ad could cause an increase in business, but you could never really know how many people actually read your ad and how many out of those came to your business because of it and made a purchase, or how many would have come anyway.

Now we have website analytics programs that allow you to ascertain every bit of information you'd ever want or need. You can easily find out how many people clicked on your affiliate link or ad and how many of those made a purchase. You can accurately determine specific conversion rates and website visitor numbers. Today is truly the best time in human history to be a marketer.

Since this is the case, it ought to be apparent to you that you'll need an easy way to make changes to your messages and your website pages and functionality to improve their marketing power. The goal is to look at your website visitor statistics regularly and make adjustments in response to what you learn.

To accomplish that, you need a fast and easy way to make changes. Be sure to ask your Web vendor to include update methods in their proposal. If they can't, then determine another way to change the content of your website before the project begins. Even if this means hiring someone to do it for you or learning how to do it yourself, it is paramount that you can make regular changes to your site once it's live.

Again, this has been only a brief description of some of the top Web marketing techniques that exist today. I have just touched the surface. You need to dig deeper, making an effort to learn more about each of these strategies from other sources.

Post-construction marketing costs are steep

If you hire a Web vendor to build you a website, and you have made no provisions for updating it or marketing it afterwards, expect to have to hire someone else and to pay more than the cost of the construction of the website.

One of the three pillars of a great website is its ongoing marketing campaigns and strategies. When you're considering hiring a Web vendor to build you a site, consider how important this is to help you make your decision. In other words, someone is going to have to market the site once it's completed. If the company you hire to design and build your site can market it as well once it's completed, and they include this service in their initial proposal, that's ideal.

If you narrow down your search to three possible Web vendors and only one of them is proficient at Web marketing, seriously consider hiring that one (all else being equal).

Conclusion

The world is moving online. By reading this book, you have made a step to move online if this is your first time, or to bring your old website to a level that will enable you to compete well and enjoy success in today's online business world.

You are now better equipped than most other people and businesses that need a new website. That's because you now understand how to hire the right Web vendor for your specific project. You know what constitutes a great website, and you know how to work with your Web team to plan and implement a successful business website.

By taking the time to read this book, you now can intelligently choose a Web vendor. You can be assured that you are not going to pay more than the service is worth. You can rest easy knowing that you did your due diligence and you can expect to get what you originally wanted and what your business really needs.

The Web is no different in most ways from the real world, and business on the Web is not different from any other type of business. They follow the same laws and principles. A website is just another tool for you to make money with your business. Indeed, it may be your only tool, so get it right the first time.

Whether you're going in for surgery, building a new home or having a baby, the more knowledge you arm yourself with in advance, the easier the process will be—and the better chance for success in the end. Hopefully this book has demystified websites and the process of finding an appropriate Web vendor for you. If you have questions about anything you've read here, do a search using your favorite search engine, and you'll most likely find the answer.

You ought to be proud of yourself for reading this book. You've put yourself way out ahead of your competition. You recognized the need for planning and the need for self-education, both of which will save you time, money and grief. Because you took the time to read this, you will most likely be the most prepared client your chosen Web vendor has ever worked with.

If I had read a book like this before I went looking for a contractor to finish our basement, I would have saved myself time and anxiety and would have been proud of the final product. (By the way, our basement is still not finished today.)

Remember the Golden Rule of website creation and management: Put yourself in the shoes of your visitors and create an experience for them that you would like to have when you visit websites. In other words, do unto them as you would like to be done to you.

Remember that the clean, simple and easy website that doesn't cause your visitors to expend priceless brain power and time unnecessarily will always win. Remember your website's primary goals for existence when making any decisions. If the site exists to make you money, always be sure you're working towards that end.

In the following appendix you'll find all the checklists, graphs and lists discussed in this book. Make copies or print them all out to begin your new Web project and Web vendor search. In the last appendix is a list of recommended books. I've read them all personally and each one contains information that will further educate you in the world of Web business. Now, as Spock used to say, "Go forth and prosper."

Appendix

The Website Plan Document

The Four Questions You Need To Answer:

> What will be the site's goals and purpose?
> Who will be your website's audience?
> What is your budget?
> What is your time frame?

Rough Website Outline

Checklists

Potential Web Vendor Website Checklist

1	Do I like the site's overall look-and-feel and design?	☐yes	☐no
2	Is it easy to navigate through the site and easy to move around in?	☐yes	☐no
3	Does the navigation make sense?	☐yes	☐no
4	Is the site free of misspellings, broken links and pages under construction?	☐yes	☐no
5	Is it easy to find any information I am looking for?	☐yes	☐no
6	Is there a list of past clients? If so, are any of them in the same industry as mine?	☐yes	☐no
7	Do I like and connect with the site's writing and content?	☐yes	☐no
8	Is there a design portfolio? If so, do I mostly like the client website designs?	☐yes	☐no

Potential Web Vendor's Client Websites Checklist

1 Have they designed, built/coded and marketed these site? ☐yes ☐no

2 Are any of these websites in the same industry as yours? ☐yes ☐no

3 Do I like each site's overall look-and-feel and design? ☐yes ☐no

4 Is it easy to navigate through each site? ☐yes ☐no

5 Does the navigation make sense? ☐yes ☐no

6 Does the navigation setup and functionality vary among sites? ☐yes ☐no

7 Are the sites free of misspellings, broken links and pages under construction? ☐yes ☐no

8 Is it easy to find any information I am looking for? ☐yes ☐no

9 Do I connect with and like the site's writing and content? ☐yes ☐no

Final Checklist

1 Does the Web vendor have design, technical, and marketing skills? ☐yes ☐no

2 Did they send a formal written proposal? ☐yes ☐no

3 Do I like their overall personality? ☐yes ☐no

4 Does it seem like they'll want to add unnecessary bells and whistles? ☐yes ☐no

5 Did they tell me where they get their images? ☐yes ☐no

6 Are they easy to get in touch with? ☐yes ☐no

7 Did they answer my emails and voice mails in a timely manner? ☐yes ☐no

8 Does the proposal contain an itemized price list? ☐yes ☐no

9 Did I get the best possible price from them? ☐yes ☐no

10 Did I get a firm end date? ☐yes ☐no

Web Vendors Comparison Chart

Vendor Name and Website	Local or Out of Town	Person Free-lancer, Sole Proprietor or Company	Did they pass their business website checklist?	Did they pass their clients' websites checklist?	How did you find them?
ABC Web Design www.abcdesign.com	Out of town	Company	Yes	Yes	Google and Yahoo
John Smith www.johnsmith.com	Out of town	Free-lancer	No	Yes	Google
Cool Designs, Inc. www.cooldesign. com	Out of town	Company	No	No	Friend recommended
Acme Development www.acmedev.com	Local	Company	Yes	yes	Business associate recommended
Ace Web Design www.acewebdesign.com	Local	Sole proprietor	Yes	Yes	Competitor used them

What to Provide the Web Vendor

The website plan document   ____

Navigation outline   ____

Content for each page   ____

Style guide   ____

Logo in digital format   ____

Website images   ____

The Great Website Qualities list   ____

Great Website Rules List

- A website needs to establish trust.

- A website needs to make the visitor's life better in some way.

- A website should offer the visitor a clean, simple and easy experience.

- A website should not make the user think unnecessarily.

- A website needs to make you and your business look professional.

- A website needs to clearly show your visitors the way to accomplishing their goals without being confusing.

- A website needs to help visitors easily find what they need and then ask them to take an action.

- A website needs to pass the AIDA test: Attention, Interest, Desire, Action.

Great Website Qualities List

Design and Content Qualities

- Uses Web conventions

- Appealing to the eye of your audience

- A look-and-feel appropriate to your subject and audience

- Consistent navigation, look-and-feel and organization
- Easy to use, easy to read
- Easily navigated and well organized
- Clear and concise navigation labels that compel people to click
- Easily searchable
- Has quality, original content that grows over time
- Well-written copy with no grammar, spelling or punctuation mistakes
- Content written for the user and not you
- Text, not just images, and text links, not just buttons
- A phone number, logo and tag line on every page

Technical Qualities

- Loads in browsers quickly
- Looks the same across platforms and browsers
- Has no broken links or images
- Never crashes
- Has form validation
- Is interactive, and the interactivity works properly
- Does not require browser plug-ins to view properly

Marketing Qualities

- Attracts first-time visitors
- Is 'sticky'—keeps the visitors from leaving
- Impels people to return later
- Obtains new leads for you regularly by building your prospect e-mail list
- Converts visitors into customers at a high rate
- Builds your brand
- Evokes emotion

- Makes sales
- Has text links to all important pages
- Has a terms and policies page
- Has a phone number or other way to contact you
- Has your business tag line
- Is search engine optimized

Recommended Reading

I have read all of the books below and I highly recommend each of them. Whether you're a Web consultant, webmaster, or small business owner whose business at least partly relies on the Web, the following books will surely help you.

Top Web Business Books

- The Death of "e" and the Birth of the Real New Economy: Business Models, Technologies and Strategies for the 21st Century - by Peter Fingar and Ronald C. Aronica
- Strategies for E-Business Success - by Erik Brynjolfsson and Glen Urban
- The Big Red Fez: How To Make Any WebSite Better - by Seth Godin
- Small Is the New Big: and 183 Other Riffs, Rants, and Remarkable Business Ideas - by Seth Godin
- Permission Marketing: Turning Strangers Into Friends And Friends Into Customers - by Seth Godin
- Call to Action: Secret Formulas to Improve Online Results - by Bryan Eisenberg, Jeffrey Eisenberg, and Lisa T. Davis
- The One to One Fieldbook - by Don Peppers, Martha Rogers, and Bob Dorf
- Web Business Engineering: Using Offline Activities to Drive Internet Strategies - by Nick V. Flor
- The AdSense Code: What Google Never Told You About Making Money with AdSense - by Joel Comm
- Place to Space: Migrating to E-business Models - by Peter Weill and Michael Vitale
- Multiple Streams of Internet Income: How Ordinary People Make Extraordinary Money Online - by Robert G. Allen
- Don't Make Me Think – by Steve Krug

Top General Business Books

- The E Myth: Why Most Small Businesses Don't Work and What to Do About It - by Michael E. Gerber
- What Clients Love: A Field Guide to Growing Your Business - by Harry Beckwith
- The 100 Absolutely Unbreakable Laws of Business Success - by Brian Tracy
- Good to Great: Why Some Companies Make the Leap... and Others Don't - by Jim Collins
- How to Make Big Money in Your Own Small Business: Unexpected Rules Every Small Business Owner Needs to Know - by Jeffrey J. Fox
- Hypnotic Writing: How to Seduce and Persuade Customers with Only Your Words - by Joe Vitale
- Influence - The Psychology of Persuasion - by Robert B. Cialdini
- Why We Buy: The Science Of Shopping - by Paco Underhill

Top Internet/Web General Books

- The Search: How Google and Its Rivals Rewrote the Rules of Business and Transformed Our Culture - by John Battelle
- Weaving the Web: The Original Design and Ultimate Destiny of the World Wide Web - by Tim Berners-Lee
- The Cluetrain Manifesto: The End of Business as Usual - by Christopher Locke

Index

Y

Blog available

I have set up a companion blog for this book at

http://www.brandonoakpublishing.com/blog

where you can leave comments and questions about this book. I want to hear from you and I will try to respond to everyone.

Also, if you liked this book and found it useful, please consider recommending it to others you know who could benefit from it as well.

Finally, consider leaving a favorable review of this book on Amazon.com. Just search for the title to locate it on Amazon.

LaVergne, TN USA
27 October 2010
202475LV00004B/34/P